ART AND
ARCHITECTURE
OF CHRISTIANITY

ART AND ARCHITECTURE OF CHRISTIANITY

Edited by Gervis Frere-Cook

THE PRESS OF CASE WESTERN RESERVE UNIVERSITY

Cleveland

1972

Frontispiece
Carne's Cross, Gloucester
Cathedral. Small limestone cross of
Celtic design carved by Colonel
Carne, VC, while a prisoner-of-
war in North Korea 1952–3.

contents

ART AND
ARCHITECTURE
OF CHRISTIANITY

chapter 1

DR JOSEPH GUTMANN

PRELUDE: THE ART OF THE JEWS

There was a time when art historians were sharply divided as to whether the origins of Christian art were to be sought in the Orient or in Rome. This issue, however, is no longer a major concern and a like fate has overtaken the once strongly advocated theory that Christian art was an independent creation. Today most scholars are agreed that, since Christianity began as an Eastern religion, the origins of its art, too, must be sought in the arts that flourished in the Near East at the time of its beginning. The Near Eastern origins of Christian art naturally suggested to scholars that Judaism and its art may have been a possible source of inspiration for the beginnings of Christian art. Amazing recent discoveries of Jewish art in the Near East, especially the third-century synagogue of Dura-Europos, seem to offer confirmation of this point of view. What is still a matter of debate, however, is the particular type of Judaism that may have served as a possible transmitter of this art to Christianity. Some scholars argue that since Pharisaic-Rabbinic Judaism was, so it is alleged, restricted by the Second Commandment, it could never have tolerated such an art; it must therefore be the product of the more liberal and assimilated Hellenistic form of Judaism. Another major controversy is the extent to which Jewish art influenced Christian art, and whether Christian art in which Jewish legendary material appears owes its derivation directly to Jewish artistic models or whether its inspiration may simply have been a Jewish or Christian literary source.

Scholars who argue that a Hellenistic Judaism served as the transmitter of Jewish art to Christianity overlook the fact that the penetration of Hellenism into the Near East, with its introduction of the Greek-type city, the polis, proved disruptive not only to Jews living outside Palestine but to those living in Palestine itself.

In major Hellenistic centres, such as Alexandria, the Pentateuch was transmuted from a Near Eastern text into a Greek text capable of coping with the needs of the polis-living Jews by endowing the simple narratives, cultic rites and laws with profound allegorical, symbolic and philosophical meanings.

In Palestine itself a new class of scholars, the Pharisees, arose

1

to solve the problems posed by Hellenism. Not satisfied with merely transmitting a Near Eastern text they set about constructing a new and radical form of Judaism. By positing a divinely revealed two-fold law, the Written and the Oral, they preserved the Pentateuch, the Written Law, while proceeding, through the Oral Law, to introduce major changes capable of mastering a Hellenistic mode of life. These revolutionary changes substituted a new Judaism centred on the scholar, the synagogue and prayer to meet the needs of the individual, replacing the old traditions of the people in their promised land who had looked towards Jerusalem and the Temple with its priestly sacrifices. Central to this new form of Judaism was the internalization of the Pharisaic laws which required, among other obligations, mandatory prayers in an unmediated relationship with God in order to secure for the individual his salvation and resurrection in the world to come. Although Christianity rejected the internalized system of laws and substituted an internalized faith in the redemptive power of Christ, the central concepts of Pharisaic Judaism—individual salvation and resurrection—remained. Hence Christianity and Christian art are deeply rooted in Pharisaic-Rabbinic Judaism and not in the early Pentateuchal or later liberal Hellenistic Judaisms.

As we would expect, therefore, the Jewish artistic remains of the early Christian period spell out on the walls and floors of synagogues—the decentralized houses of worship introduced by the Pharisees—their new salvationary message and not the mystic symbolism of the Hellenistic Jews as some scholars suggest. In the Dura-Europos synagogue, in particular, we find that the 'Old Testament' is used, analagously, as a proof text to underwrite the new theological thought system of Pharisaic-Rabbinic Judaism, just as Christian monuments were somewhat later to employ the 'Old Testament' in analogous terms to spell out the Christian message of salvation.

Did the specific paintings or their immediate models on the walls of the Dura-Europos synagogue exert an influence on later Christian art, as some scholars maintain? If we compare the 'Sacrifice of Isaac' as depicted in the Dura synagogue with that in a twelfth-century Christian Octateuch miniature we find in both that the ram is not entangled in a thicket but tied to a tree and that the hand of God, and not an angel, intervenes to stop the deed. In the same way the 'Anointing of David' as seen in the Dura synagogue and in the ninth-century Paris Psalter differs from the biblical account by showing only six brothers present instead of seven. Yet again the 'Vision of Ezekiel' portrayed in the Dura synagogue and in the ninth-century East Christian miniature introduce into the scene a cleft Mount of Olives, which is not described in the Bible. While these iconographic parallels, based on rabbinic interpretations of biblical accounts, exist between the Dura frescoes and later Christian art, there are few stylistic similarities that are sufficiently convincing to warrant the conclusion that Jewish artistic models, such as the Dura synagogue frescoes, necessarily influenced later Christian artistic examples.

Some scholars argue that medieval Jewish art preserved early Jewish models which can help us establish and study the sources of early Christian art. They feel, for instance, that the depiction of the Tabernacle-Temple vessels in early Christian art can be understood only by examining the unbroken chain of tradition of such depictions stretching from early synagogue

2

2

1, 2 Abraham prepares for the sacrifice of Isaac. In the fresco in the Dura-Europos Synagogue the story is to one side of the Temple portico and is counterbalanced by the great seven-branched candlestick: the manuscript illustration is from the twelfth-century text of the Octateuch. In both the hand of God can clearly be seen restraining Abraham from the sacrifice of his son

3 The anointing of David. Fresco in the Dura-Europos Synagogue

mosaics into medieval Hebrew manuscripts. However, a close examination of the sixth-century synagogue mosaic of Beth-Alpha, for instance, reveals that there is no such chain of Jewish artistic tradition which can be used to study early Christian art. The Beth-Alpha mosaic clearly depicts the synagogal Torah ark flanked by the symbols of the Jewish holidays and not the vessels in the Tabernacle-Temple. While these vessels do sometimes appear in later Hebrew manuscripts, as in the illustration from a tenth-century Pentateuch, they show few analogies to the objects depicted in the synagogue mosaics.

In another attempt to demonstrate that medieval Jewish art preserved earlier Jewish artistic models, some scholars have noted that the Egyptian princess in a fourteenth-century

Spanish Hebrew manuscript is shown nude, as she is in the Dura synagogue fresco. In this particular instance, however, we find that the immediate source of inspiration for the unusually fourteenth-century Jewish depiction was not the fresco but a twelfth-century Spanish Christian miniature of the scene.

Many Christian works of art are assumed by scholars to be based on lost earlier Jewish models, since they incorporate Jewish legendary material. Examples include a depiction of the serpent in the Garden of Eden which has mounted a camel-like creature, thereby giving the appearance of having four legs; the raven sent forth by Noah seen feeding upon the body of a dead man (appearing in the thirteenth-century San Marco mosaic, which, like the Octateuchs, is based on earlier models);

3

Joseph encountering the winged Gabriel while on his way to find his brethren, and Benjamin sitting next to his brother Joseph at the meal they eat together in Egypt. These non-biblical Jewish legendary accounts, reflected in Christian works, constitute insufficient evidence to establish the existence of lost ancient Jewish manuscripts. Since many of these same Jewish legends appear also in the patristic writings, it may well be that a Christian source, rather than a Jewish, inspired their creation.

There is no doubt that the beginnings of Christian art and its distinct message of salvation cannot be properly evaluated without an understanding of the revolutionary changes introduced by Pharisaic-Rabbinic Judaism. Whether early Jewish art of this period was a major factor in stimulating and influencing early Christian art must, at the present state of research, remain an open question.

4 *The anointing of David. From a ninth-century psalter*

5, 6 *The vision of Ezekiel as depicted in the Dura-Europos Synagogue and by contrast in a ninth-century miniature. This, like (4), is far more ornate than the fresco*

7 *The Torah Ark. This mosaic from the Synagogue of Beth-Alpha is flanked by the symbols of the Jewish holidays*

8 *By comparison with (7) this picture of the Tabernacle-Temple from a tenth-century Pentateuch shows the central items supported by the vessels used in the Temple*

9–11 *Three pictures illustrating the finding of Moses by Pharaoh's daughter*

9 *Fresco in the Dura-Europos Synagogue*

10 *From a fourteenth-century Spanish–Hebrew manuscript*

11 *From a twelfth-century Spanish–Christian manuscript*

8

7

12 *The serpent beguiles Eve in the Garden of Eden. Twelfth-century Octateuch miniature*

13 *Noah sends forth the dove from the Ark while the raven feeds on the body of a drowned man. Thirteenth-century mosaic*

14 *Joseph encounters the angel Gabriel. Sixth-century manuscript*

15 *Joseph places his brother Benjamin next to him at table. Seventh-century Ashburnham Pentateuch*

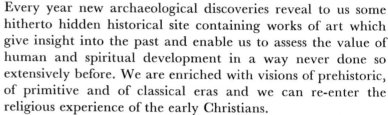

chapter 2

JOAN MORRIS M.A.

THE FIRST PORTRAYAL

Every year new archaeological discoveries reveal to us some hitherto hidden historical site containing works of art which give insight into the past and enable us to assess the value of human and spiritual development in a way never done so extensively before. We are enriched with visions of prehistoric, of primitive and of classical eras and we can re-enter the religious experience of the early Christians.

Burial-grounds have proved to be exceptionally good places for finding untouched examples of early Christian art. The catacombs in Rome, Naples, Ravenna, Arles, Syracuse, Algiers, Alexandria and other cities in the East have been excavated continuously during the last one hundred and fifty years and they are well known for their frescoes and sculptured sarcophagi, which by their similarity show that from the beginning a pictorial system was established to convey the faith and to awaken hope in a future life through unity in Jesus Christ, Son of God.

The discovery of the Dura-Europos church-house, with a baptistry fully decorated, dating from AD 256, convinces us of the unity of doctrine taught in places far distant from each other in the East and in the West.

The Good Shepherd was the favourite way of representing Christ as Saviour, carrying the lost sheep on his shoulder, often accompanied by the figure of a woman orante, representing His Spouse the Church, with hands outstretched in prayer for the departed soul. In some paintings the Good Shepherd holds a small pot in one hand corresponding to the idea expressed in the second-century Eastern epitaph, in which the defunct Abercius declares himself to be 'the disciple of the Good Shepherd who feeds his lambs on the mountains and on the plains', so alluding to the spiritual food of the Eucharist. Often the Good Shepherd is placed within a vine-tree decoration, the symbolic sign of sacrifice in the Eucharist, recalling the words of Christ himself: 'I am the Good Shepherd: the Good Shepherd giveth his life for the sheep' (John 10, 11).

An Eastern example of the Good Shepherd was found on the back wall of the baptistry of the church-house at Dura, and this painting has been restored and preserved in a reconstructed edifice in the Damascus Museum, whilst Asia Minor has several among its funeral monuments. Representations of the Good Shepherd were even more popular in the West. In Rome it is an oft-repeated theme and it also occurs on many sarcophagi in Arles and Ravenna. In Africa, too, it was common and in the Soussa catacombs there is a fine second-century example. Here the shepherd has bare legs and feet and is evidently not copied from a Roman example. The great popularity of the theme is shown by the many medallions, gems, glass bowls, lamps and other objects bearing representations of the Good Shepherd. Later the theme was developed in large compositions such as the Galla Placida Mausoleum apsidál mosaic in Ravenna and in modern times Picasso has returned to the same subject.

Early realistic representations of Christ portray Him as a young man without a beard, in contrast to the heavily bearded Apostles beside Him. It seems to suggest that Christ as God was perennially young. Again, this type of portrayal was common in the East and in the West. The chalice of Antioch, which consists of an inner cup preserved within a richly worked silver container, shows Christ as a young man, together with bearded Apostles, seated within entwining vine branches. Similarly the figure of Christ on many of the sarcophagi in Rome, Gaul and elsewhere, portray Him as young and beardless with bearded Apostles around Him.

Old Testament stories as prototypes of New Testament events prevailed in all early Christian centres and have continued through many centuries. The sacrifice of Isaac by Abraham, standing for the sacrifice of Jesus Christ the Son of God, is still commonly used today. Perhaps the most often-repeated subject is the story of Jonah and the whale, mentioned by Christ Himself as a type of His resurrection. The sequence of events is nearly always given in the same order: the throwing of Jonah out of the ship, the whale waiting to devour him, the vomiting of Jonah on to the seashore and finally his state of bliss under the shadow of the vine, signifying paradise. Other common prototypes are Elijah going up in his chariot to the skies, a forerunner of the Ascension, while the Tower of Babel stands for the chaos of the confusion of tongues by contrast with the gift of tongues at Pentecost and the resultant harmony. The fifteenth-century book, *Speculum Humanae Salvatoris*, translated into many languages and illustrated by different artists, has preserved for us the whole set of Old Testament prefigurements painted side by side with New Testament events. The 'Dittochaeon', short poems by Prudentius in the fourth century, describe Old and New Testament scenes in historical sequence, written it is believed for mosaic workers, and such a sequence is also to be found around the nave of the Basilica of Santa Maria Maggiore, Rome.

The sign of the cross scratched or carved on stone was used in a variety of forms from early times. The Greek letter *tau*, 'T', is found in several galleries of the second-century Soussa Catacombs. The anchor signifying the cross is also found there as in the catacombs of Priscilla where it is connected with the word *elpis* meaning hope. The Ancient Egyptian ankh stood for eternal life and was converted into the Christian symbol for the cross; so was the pre-Christian Swatziger cross. The *chi-rho*, the first two Greek letters in the name of Christ, became used as a form of cross and was made popular in the Constantine Monogram where it is placed in the centre of the laurel wreath denoting victory, commemorating Constantine's victory after his vision at the Milvian Bridge, after which Christianity was

MVNIFICENTIA. LEONIS. XIII. P. M.

adopted as a state religion. The alpha and omega, 'A' and 'Ω', the first and last letters of the Greek alphabet, referred to in the twenty-first chapter of the Book of the Revelation in which Christ declares Himself to be Alpha and Omega, the beginning and the end, led to the use of these letters on paintings and they were hung on crosses, sometimes also with a fish. The word *Ichthus*, Greek for a fish, was used as an acrostic Ἰχθυς, each letter being the initial letter of the words Ἰησους Χριστος Θεου Ὑιος Ξωτηρ, Jesus Christ, of God the Son, Saviour.

The figure of Christ hanging on the cross was not depicted until after the abolition of crucifixion as a form of execution by Constantine following the recognition of Christianity in AD 313. We have an example of a fourth-century crucifixion with a nude figure of Christ on an ivory casket in the British Museum, whilst in some instances the figure was robed and also crowned in glory, signifying the victory of the cross.

All early representations of the Last Supper show Our Lord and the Apostles reclining round a central table in a horse-shoe shape. The 'Last Supper' of Leonardo da Vinci is an anachronism; there was certainly no long, high table. The custom of reclining gives the whole scene much greater intimacy and makes the gesture of John leaning against the side of Christ much more understandable. In the Chapel of the Sacraments in the catacombs of St Callixtus a fresco depicts the early celebration of the Eucharist. There are baskets of loaves evoking the miracle of the multiplication of loaves by Our Lord in the desert and there are flagons of wine recalling the turning of water into wine at the marriage feast of Cana, both awakening faith in the Eucharistic Sacraments. Above to the right is the sacrifice of Isaac by Abraham, and to the left there is a man stretching out his hands over a tripod table with a dish and a fish upon it, and an orante by the side, confirming the Eucharistic subject-matter of the whole wall.

Redemption through baptism was often rendered in pictorial form, as in the ivory casket of the Maskel Collection in the British Museum which conveys the thought in four ivory miniatures.

The earliest known representation of the Virgin Mary is the second-century fresco in the catacombs of Priscilla, Rome. A prophet to the left of the mother and child is pointing to a star above, generally considered to be Isaiah foretelling the coming of the Messiah: 'Arise, shine out, for your light has come, the glory of Yahweh is given you' or he may perhaps be Micah prophesying the birth at Bethlehem. By the third century the Virgin is already in a central position facing forwards and presenting the Child Jesus, and there are a considerable number of Nativity scenes giving the full story on fourth-century sarcophagi. The Ascension scene on the pilgrimage souvenir flasks,

brought from Jerusalem as a present to Queen Theodolina by Pope Gregory the Great, show the Virgin Mary in the centre with a halo, but not so the Apostles surrounding her. A much later Ethiopian manuscript does the same but the Coptic sixth-century frescoes of the Ascension at Bawit show the Virgin either standing or enthroned with Apostles in order on either side, and all have haloes, whilst a Ravenna ivory plaque presents her enthroned with angels on either side.

Whilst the cultural basis of Christian thought in literary form was mainly Greco-Roman and Hebrew the source in the visual arts was principally Syrian. Syria, however, was subject to influence from the East and from the West, from Persia and from Rome, and Syrian art is didactic rather than decorative. The Rabulla Gospel Book, now in Florence, is an outstanding example. It is a Syrian manuscript copied by a monk called Rabulla from the monastery of Mar John Zagbae in Mesopotamia. The fourteen miniatures included show both Persian and Greco-Roman influence, the Persian being decorative and flat, the Greco-Roman more modelled.

By contrast the Hellenistic influence was more refined, depicting idealistic human figures, men and horses with tapered extremities, drapery arranged in well-designed folds, as seen in the Joshua Rolls, an Alexandrian manuscript of the fifth century. Alexandria, the centre of Christian Hellenistic culture, was destroyed by Arabic wars so our knowledge of that important period is impaired.

The Copts, Egyptian Christians, were opposed to the Greeks in Alexandria and were influenced by Syrian rather than Hellenistic culture. The Copts were from the working classes, not the intellectual, and they were looked down upon by the Greek Egyptians; but it was the Copts who produced the monks and nuns in the desert and who constructed the monasteries. Coptic art retains some elements of Ancient Egyptian art, though less than might be expected. The ankh cross was used as already mentioned and the Ancient Egyptian textile designs were adapted to Christian subjects and have been found in Christian tombs where the custom of mummifying the dead has been abandoned. The Copts did not build in granite as the Ancient Egyptians did, but used a softer limestone resulting in a less polished and rougher style. Their favourite saints were Tecla and Menas, both showing Syrian and Asia Minor derivation. The frescoes, too, are painted in a thick sturdy line and are vigorous rather than refined.

The Ethiopian Church, a branch of the Coptic and Monophysite Church of Alexandria, after being cut off by the Arabic wars in the sixth century, withstood Islamic influence and continued to develop independently, looking upon Jerusalem as the home and source of religion and claiming descent from King

Solomon and the Queen of Sheba. In church architecture they used a pre-Christian Ethiopic style. The Dabro Damo cliff monastery, which can be reached only by climbing a rope, is constructed with alternate wood and stone layers as at the pagan mausoleum of Aksum. Of special interest are the many rock-hewn churches, eleven in the sacred town of Lalibala alone. These are carved out of the rock and are freed on all sides. The Mariam Church, the finest of the Lalibala monoliths, has sculptured reliefs of life-sized effigies of the saints on the exterior walls. The monasteries, situated on isolated islands in Lake Tana and Lake Taig, became important spiritual centres and produced an enormous number of manuscripts, many profusely illustrated. Those extant date only from the fourteenth century, though earlier examples must have existed. During the fourteenth and fifteenth centuries the subjects were chiefly biblical; the four Gospels and the Epistles of St Paul. Christ and the Apostles are usually represented bare-headed with black hair and beards, and they have haloes, whereas the Scribes and Pharisees are depicted with a variety of Jewish-styled hats and turbans. The faces in this period are long and thin like the Ethiopians themselves, but after the arrival of the Portuguese the heads became rounded and the subjects of the books changed to the lives of Mary and the saints. The second Islamic invasion of 1527–43 again destroyed many churches and monasteries, but again the invasions had the effect of cutting off Ethiopia from European influence and caused the Ethiopians to maintain their own specific religious culture expressed in dance, poetry and painting, so preserving an early Christian tradition right up to our own times.

The 'Thousand and One Churches' of Asia Minor, damaged and lost by many wars, of which we have only archaeological remains described for us by Ramsay and Bell, demonstrate the profusion of Christian life that once existed in these parts. By literary reference in the Chronicles of Arbela we know that Edessa and Nisibi already had churches in the second century. The theological schools of these cities developed the iconographic cycles familiar to us in the rock-churches of Cappadocia. The 'Guide to Painters' found by Didron on Mount Athos, though a late work, is based on these early iconographic schemes which were complete and extensive expositions of the Christian faith.

The Armenian Church branched off from the Cappadocian Church and at first maintained independence from the eastern Mazdean influence. The Church of Acthamar on Lake Van is exceptional for its sculptured façades. Though these date as late as the tenth century the subjects recall Dura and the Roman catacombs: Jonah addressing the Ninevites; David and Goliath; the three youths in the furnace; all show Syrian influence.

Armenia developed its own style of illuminations. One strange feature is the often-repeated portrayal of a human figure with an animal head, or three heads, of which one is animal. It may refer to King Tiridates who is said to have become like an animal after causing the martyrdom of St Rhipsime and her companions until his later conversion by St Gregory the Illuminator. Later, like the rest of Christendom, Armenia came under the influence of Byzantine art.

All these various art cultures, through the pilgrims who gathered around the holy places in Jerusalem, reacted upon one another and assisted in creating a united Christian front which radiated out to the east and to the west. This unity was ruptured in later centuries, but early Christian art testifies to no fundamental difference between East and West, but on the contrary to a very fruitful partnership.

2

3, 4 *A faint wall-carving from the second-century catacombs at Soussa in Africa and the funeral monument from Asia Minor show how widely spread was the concept of the Good Shepherd*

5 *The Chalice of Antioch. A fourth-century silver reliquary cup 7½ in. high, part of the silver being gilded*

6 *This wonderfully carved ivory book-cover shows the beardless Christ with bearded apostl on each side. At the top two angels hold the cross in a wreath of laurel while at the bottom is related the story of Jonah and the great fish Immediately below the central carving an ange rescues Shadrach, Meshak and Abednego from the fiery furnace. At each side a pair of miracle are depicted: the raising of Lazarus; the healin of the sick of the palsy: the restoring of sight to the blind man; and the casting out of a dev*

5

7

7 *Another carved ivory book-cover, this time showing scenes from the Nativity*

8 *The catacomb wall-paintings have inevitably suffered badly with the passage of time. This one from the third century shows the sacrifice of Isaac*

9 *By contrast with the wall-painting this carved sarcophagus of the same period, which tells the story of Jonah, is marvellously preserved*

10 *The Rabulla Gospel Book of the seventh century is of Syrian origin and this picture of the Ascension shows the merging of the styles of the East and West*

8

9

11, 12 *Here again the theme of Jonah is repeated on the walls of the Armenian Church of Acthanar. The view of the east end shows the wealth of high relief carving*

13 *Contrasting adjacent pictures from the fifteenth century illuminated manuscript Speculum Humanae Salvatoris show the confusion of the Tower of Babel and the harmony of Pentecost*

14 *The Constantine Monogram with the* chi-rho *symbol of the cross, from the fourth-century chapel in Lullingstone, Kent*

11

12

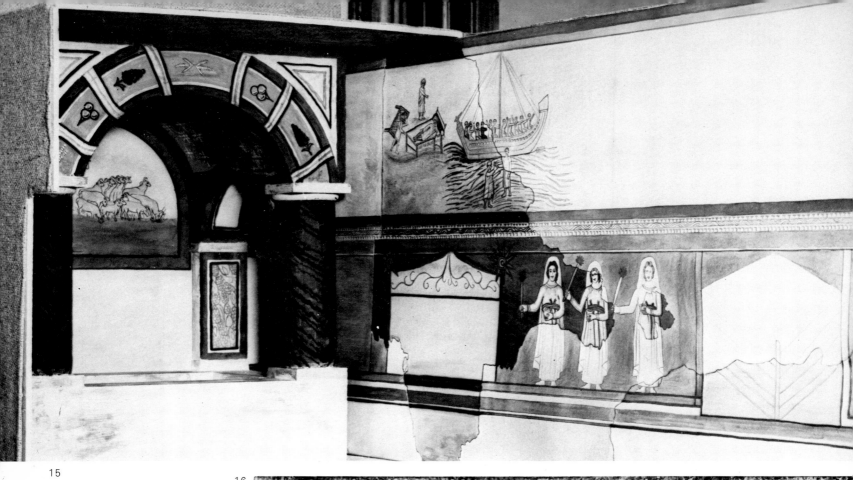

15

16

20

15 *Reconstruction in the Damascus Museum of the Baptistry of the Church House at Dura. The Good Shepherd theme can be partially seen in the apse while the wall frescoes depict miracles and the parable of the wise virgins*

16 *This mosaic from the Soussa Catacomb, Africa, depicts the anchor of salvation through the cross of Christ, represented by the fish*

17 *The Last Supper. Fresco from the Catacomb of St Callixtus*

18 *The Ankh Cross: a piece of Coptic sculpture. The Ankh was the symbol of eternal life in the art of Ancient Egypt and was modified to form a Christian cross*

19 *Ivory crucifixion from an early Christian casket of the fourth century, with Judas Iscariot hanging to one side*

18

19

20 (overleaf) *The Virgin Mary and Child Jesus with a prophet pointing to a star above foretelling the birth of the Messiah. This fresco from the Catacomb of St Priscilla is the earliest known representation of the Virgin*

21 (overleaf) *The Ascension, from the Kebran MS, is from a fifteenth-century Ethiopian book and shows the Virgin Mary with a halo, but not the Apostles, a throw-back to an earlier practice*

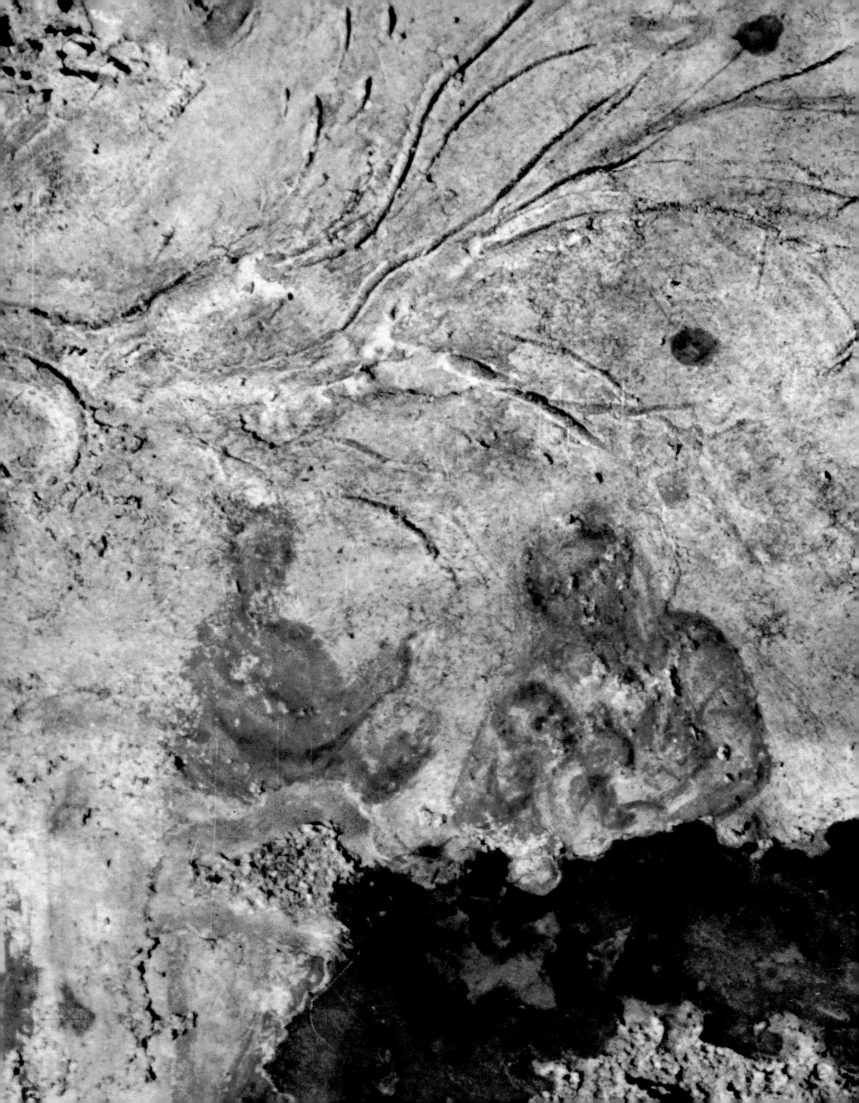

22 *The Ascension. Fresco from the Coptic Bawit Monastery showing the Virgin Mary and Apostles, all with haloes*

23 *Crucifixion scene from a door panel in the Church of S. Sabina, Rome; fifth century*

22 23

24

a

c   d

b

24 *Baptismal casket of carved ivory depicting:*
  (a) *Moses touching the rock and water flowing out, foreshadowing baptism*
  (b) *The raising of Tabitha to life by Peter, evoking faith in the new life by baptism*
  (c) *Tecla and Paul conversing together. Tecla had a mission to baptize, a task performed by deaconesses during the first millennium*
  (d) *The stoning of Paul, showing how we die together with Christ in baptism so that as He rose we may also have newness of life*

25 *The Virgin and Child. Third-century fresco from the Roman catacombs*

26 *The Ascension, as shown on the Monza flask brought to Queen Theodolina by Pope Gregory the Great*

27 *Elijah ascending into Heaven in his chariot; door panel in the Church of S. Sabina*

26

27

28 *The Entombment: from the Kebran MS*

29 *The Descent from the Cross. From the Ethiopian Gospel Book*

29

30

30 *The Hellenistic influence in art can be seen in this picture from the Joshua Rolls, an Alexandrian MS of the fifth century*

31 *Pentecost fresco from the Cappadocian Church of Kiliçlar*

31

chapter 3

E. R. CHAMBERLIN

MONASTERY AND CATHEDRAL

THE MONASTERY

Shortly after the turn of the millennium Brother Raoul, nicknamed the Bald—monk, gossiper and chronicler—turned his attention from the wars of kings to remark upon a curious cultural phenomenon—the sudden upsurge of great abbey churches. 'It seemed as though all the world were throwing off its slumber to clothe itself anew in white sanctuaries. Everywhere, people began to restore the churches and, though many were still in good condition, they vied with each other in erecting new buildings, each one more beautiful than the last.'

The tendency today is to play down the once fashionable view that all Europe dwelt in terror of the approach of AD 1000, the year that would mark the Second Coming of Christ. It is doubtless true that most Europeans continued to jog along much as they had done over the past thousand years, the ordinary cycle of war, famine, plague being sufficient to preoccupy most men. But there were many who looked upon AD 1000 as being something considerably out of the ordinary. 'Seeing that the End of the World is approaching' is a common formula in late tenth-century legal texts. Wandering friars took the theme of the imminence of Anti-Christ as ideal material for their hell-fire sermons. There was even a date assigned—when the Annunciation (25 March) should fall upon Good Friday. The great theme which appears again and again in stone, paint, or on vellum is the Apocalypse, that fevered dream of a day of wrath. The 'array of white sanctuaries' which dazzled Raoul Glaber about the year 1040 was either planned or commenced about the millennium, strong enough evidence of a highly charged emotional atmosphere. Glaber at least linked their appearance with the sense of relief that the world had not been destroyed.

The date was arbitrary but the fact of change was real: Europe was stirring from a long and troubled half-sleep. The darkness of the Dark Ages has been rendered less impenetrable in recent years. Archaeologists and archivists alike have succeeded in throwing light over much of its course to show that, during the centuries-long period between the final extinction of the Roman Empire and the appearance of identifiable nation-states, though Europe had lost social cohesion it had not slumped back into savagery. Art, sure index to a society's mind, shows an admittedly confused but immensely vigorous period whose vitalities were dispersed through many channels. Gradually, those channels found their way into one great stream, the Romanesque—that massive style of architecture which took its plan from the basilicas of Rome but whose elevation perfectly expressed its time. Raoul Glaber's white buildings were as much castles as sanctuaries: Europe was still a fragmented, embattled society groping for unity through the Universal Church.

Throughout the twelfth century this most suprahuman of religious styles dominated. It was, perhaps, more truly international than the succeeding Gothic, even though its regional styles could vary from the mosaiced blaze of the Venetian and Sicilian cathedrals to the gloomy strength of the Norman. It was a style uninfluenced by humanism: the elongated figures sculptured on the portals, with their remote, austere faces, inspire awe rather than affection. Christ appears as Creator and Judge: the Child is yet to come. In all its ramifications—from engineering to illumination, in stone, brick, vellum, or glass, Romanesque art is the working out of a theology more Oriental than Occidental. Byzantium is still the great Christian centre for Rome is still plunged in its long night and Paris still fighting for dominance.

The internationalism of Romanesque was essentially an expression of that great international institution, the monastery, which largely created it. The monastery was one of the units of the feudal structure which imposed an order upon the chaos of the dark centuries; the abbot was lord of his manor, equal in rights to his lay equivalent, the baron. But, unlike the baron, he was directly linked to the head of the Universal Church and, in those centuries, the Pope was a temporal Power to be reckoned with. The monastery therefore enjoyed considerable independence.

For centuries there was only one monastic Order through Europe, the Benedictine. In the tenth century vigorous reform from within, originating in Cluny, began to transform the corrupt religious institution into an enormously powerful organization which was to have profound social and economic effects upon Europe. Benedict, saint and mystic though he was, knew too well that few men could hope to maintain spiritual health in a life of pure contemplation and had wisely emphasized the need for manual labour in a religious community. From the beginning, his monasteries formed vital economic units. Daughter houses were established in the wilder parts of the country. Secure within the great buildings raised by their own hands, protected from the lawless by their religious nature, the communities gradually tamed the land around them. Wilderness was turned into farmland: villages grew up around the monastery and a chain of civilized oases was built across the continent.

Much of what the monasteries performed in the field of learning has been exaggerated. They were primarily religious institutions and their teaching was largely limited to the learning by rote of the sacred offices, the Bible and the works of the Fathers of the Church. But, until the establishment of the cathedral schools in the late twelfth century which, in turn, gave birth to the universities, it was in the monasteries that the sum of learning was contained. The Church's intellectual life was centred around a handful of sacred texts and it was the production of these manuscripts which was the monasteries' main contribution to learning.

The freedom of the monastery from economic pressure perfectly suited it to the laborious task of endless copying which was the only possible method of book production until Gutenberg's invention in the fifteenth century. Benedictine monasteries were built to a standard pattern and part of that standardization was the scriptoria. One wall of the cloisters would be given over to a series of little wooden cubicles—carrells—where the scribe would pass his days in a space just large enough to hold his lectern and a shelf or two for inks and pens. Other monastic Orders, as they came into existence, evolved their own system of scriptoria, the aristocratic Carthusians even setting aside a cell complete with little garden for their favoured scribes. But the Benedictine system was ideally suited to that mass production of manuscripts which, in the late thirteenth century, produced most of the surviving ninety-odd manuscripts of the Apocalypse, as well as many thousands of the great Vulgate Bibles.

The first great period of northern manuscripts was a product of that hybrid culture now termed Anglo-Norman which, in the opening decades of the thirteenth century, gave England a brief artistic pre-eminence in Europe. But though artists worked under the patronage of English kings it was a genuine fusion of cultures. In the field of manuscripts it is virtually impossible to classify any particular work as a specifically French or English product. The artist might be French-born and French-speaking, yet he might be at work in Winchester or Canterbury, Norwich or Bury St Edmunds. By the end of the century, however, clear-cut national characteristics begin to appear and from the fourteenth century onwards the centre of production shifted to France—particularly Paris. This was the period of the sumptuously illuminated manuscript, itself a herald of decline, when lay-workers began to infiltrate the scriptoria. Significantly, it is a layman, Pol di Limbourg, and his brother Jean, who produced at the turn of the fourteenth century two of the most famous of illuminated manuscripts—the gorgeous Books of Hours for the wealthy dilettante, the Duke of Berry, which take their titles from casual entries in an inventory of 'Très Riches Heures' and the 'Belles Heures'. Thereafter, the illuminated manuscript increasingly became an article of profit and, in consequence, began to suffer debasement.

THE CATHEDRAL

The monastery had developed in a still rural Europe: the cathedral came as the crown of an urban community. Throughout the Continent, cities were asserting their corporate identities. Burghers, grown rich with increasing trade and learning the priceless lesson of co-operation, created a series of virtual city-states which fiercely defended their rights even against their nominal overlords. The cathedral was the seat of the bishop—but it was also the glory of the city, and chroniclers again and again record astonishing scenes when nobles and burghers joined with the disfranchised poor to labour together on the site of their city's cathedral. Money was always running short but appeals were rarely made to the citizens in vain. The bishop, too, though part of the Roman hierarchy, defended his rights against the Holy See as fiercely as the burghers defended theirs against the king. The great tussles of the age, indeed, are as frequent between pope and bishop as between pope and monarch. In France, particularly, the independence and arrogance of the bishops at one point seemed about to create a national, Gallic, Church.

The monastery expressed itself in Romanesque: the cathedral in Gothic. This all-embracing term is of comparatively recent date. Raphael used it, pejoratively, in the sixteenth century and it passed into England, still in the contemptuous mode, via Sir Henry Wotton. Evelyn followed him and the great authority of Christopher Wren established it firmly. But then, beginning with Horace Walpole, there began the romantic reaction in its favour. The reaction obscured its essential nature as thoroughly as the contemptuous assessment of the Renaissance, culminating in the 'Gothic' of Victorian England when psalters were illuminated by chromo-lithography and produced on steam presses. Even as late as 1888 the great Ninth Edition of the *Encyclopædia Britannica* is uncertain as to what term to use for the architecture, deciding at last, though hesitantly, for the noncommittal phrase 'Pointed-Architecture'.

There was no doubt as to what contemporary Europeans considered to be the origins of the style: they called it 'French work'. It was in the Île de France that, some time during the twelfth century, there was evolved that pointed arch which was to alter the whole scale and nature of religious architecture and, with it, religious art.

But there was more to Gothic than an engineering innovation. The thirteenth century, which brought the form to its height was, above all, the century of the intellect. It was the century of Dante and Aquinas and of the encyclopædists: the century when logic was subordinate to theology alone. The movement began in France for a very good reason. 'France is the oven wherein is baked the bread for the human mind,' declared Cardinal Eudes de Chateaurouge, and, though he was a Frenchman he spoke truly enough, for in the schools clustered round the towering new cathedrals of Paris and Rheims, Chartres and Angers was hammered out the system that strove to unite the great pagan philosophers with the Christian Fathers, to reconcile Aristotle with Augustine, Plato with Jerome. And a manifestation of this energy was the art-form which Renaissance Italians, preoccupied with their classic models, were to stigmatize as barbaric—the art of the Goths.

The first truly Gothic building was an abbey church—that raised over the shrine of St Denis, patron of France. The Abbey of Saint-Denis was under the direct protection of the Kings of France and its great abbot, Suger, was not only priest but statesman, intimate councillor of the King. Under his energetic and personal direction a vast new building arose so swiftly that it was dedicated, in 1144, in his own lifetime. Saint-Denis contained much of the Romanesque but it contained, too, all the features which identify Gothic—the pointed arch which takes roof thrust down to foundations, the intimate sculpture, and, above all, the great windows of stained glass. He himself appears in one of these living jewels and fittingly so, for it needed both courage and foresight to plan what were virtually glass walls. 'The great church windows are the Divine writings that let the light of the true Sun—that is to say, God—into the church—that is to say, the hearts of the faithful.'

The Romanesque artist had taken for his text the Old Testament with its remote and austere figures: the Gothic artist took the New. The vivid parables of Christ allowed the introduction of the common man, his beasts, his implements of work. Christ, who had been a carpenter, would not be offended by the appearance of carpenters in His house—or of butchers or fishmongers, peasants or merchants. All find their place—subordinate to the great mysteries of the Incarnation and the Resurrection, but still honoured—in what appears to be a riot of iconography but is in fact the result of a planned, didactic system.

It was the master mason who was responsible, as far as any one man could be responsible, for the direction of labour which produced the thousands of sculptured details in the cathedral's

'building hut'. He would have begun his career as a stone-mason but, after his apprenticeship, an ambitious man would travel from one cathedral site to another and when at last he was entrusted with his own hut he would have the skills of half a dozen trades at his finger-tips. The sculptors beneath him were classed as simple masons but they, of necessity, were artists of a high order. Massed with the work of their fellows, their products merge into the building: detached, and they can be seen for what they are—individual works of art always of a high, and frequently of a superb, class. The sculptors of the haunting 'Le Beau Dieu' of Amiens, of the tragic grace of the 'Synagogue' of Bamberg, of the 'Smiling Angel' of Rheims were men capable of standing beside any of the publicized figures of the High Renaissance.

The artist neither expected nor desired freedom in the modern sense. Away from the graphic arts, his approach is very much of a living tradition being analogous to the role of an actor in a classic drama. No one expects a modern Hamlet to introduce new lines or a different ending to the play: the course of the drama is utterly predictable in every performance—it is in the interpretation of detail that the actor's skill lies. So, too, for many centuries, was the role of the artist in any medium. His subject-matter was strictly limited by a tradition which had become sacred, for it was contained in one or other of the two great feasts of the Church—the Nativity and the Passion. Each saint had to have his or her immediately recognizable attributes and even the colour of robes would be specified.

One of the clearest possible examples of the degree of control to which an artist could be subjected is that shown in a contract between a certain Enguerrand de Quarton, painter, and Jean de Montignac, priest, for a painting of the Coronation of the Virgin. The date of the contract is 1453—the same year in which Constantinople fell and which, in modern canons, marks the opening of the Renaissance and the modern world. Yet Quarton's contract could have been drawn up at almost any date of the preceding thousand years, so minutely does it specify both treatment and subject. Father Montignac obviously wanted to tread very carefully around that aspect of the Trinity expressed in the Creed where the Son is defined as being of the same substance as the Father. 'There shall not be any difference between Father and Son', he lays down firmly, and Quarton obliges by creating two figures who could be twin brothers. He is further instructed that the Trinity was to place the crown on the Virgin—that is, all three Persons were to unite in crowning one. It could have led to a slightly ludicrous effect had he not made use of the convention whereby a dove signifies the Holy Spirit. Instead of a confused central mass he is thus able to flank the main figure with two others while a bird

3 *'Man, God and Devil'. The Creator looks compassionately upon the corpse while the Archangel battles with the Devil for his soul*. Rohan Book of Hours

hovers gracefully overhead. He is given a list of saints who are to appear, instructed to place Rome upon the Tiber which, in turn, must enter the sea and beyond the sea must be shown the Holy Land with the Mount of Olives. Curiously, he is given a free hand with the peopling of Hell which will contain 'all the estates according to the judgement of Master Enguerrand'. Doubtless he enjoyed himself there, as all medieval artists did, Hell being a far more interesting subject than Heaven with its monotony of chanting saints. But, lest he should go too far, the contract ends cautiously with the warning that 'throughout, he shall be guided by his conscience'.

Enguerrand de Quarton's painting, produced to a precise formula, is not noticeably inferior to many thousands of productions whose creators are limited only by their talent.

2

3

5 'Coronation of the Virgin'. Enguerrand de Quarton

6

7 8

6 'The Triumph of Death'. From the Campo Santo, Pisa, probably painted by Andrea and Nardo Orcagna. Three young men, out for a day's sport, come across their own corpses

7, 8 Details from 'The Triumph of Death'. While devils carry the damned to Hell in one scene, in another corner two aged monks peruse a holy book

9, 10 Carved scenes from the Last Judgement on the west façade of Bourges Cathedral. The chosen are led by St Peter towards Paradise whilst elsewhere St Michael weighs a soul in the balance: the small boy calmly awaits the verdict but the devil seems quite happy that he will soon enough have a victim

12

13 'Paradise', by Andrea Orcagna in the Church of S. Maria Novella, Florence

14 The Cloisters of Gloucester Cathedral

15 Dedication of the third Abbey of Cluny. It was here that the great Benedictine reform was begun in the tenth and eleventh centuries. Abbott Hugh is in the centre

14

15

+ SCRIPTOR ⁊ SRIPTORVM PRINCEPS EGO NEC OBITVRA DEINCEPS LAVS MEA NEC FAMA QVISSIM

16 *Eadwine of Christchurch, Canterbury, from his own psalter*

17 *Portrait bust of Peter Parler, master mason at Prague where he took over in 1353. The medieval artist was essentially anonymous and there was no distinction between artist and craftsman. Sometimes, however, an identified figure appears, most commonly in manuscripts as an elaborate doodle in the margin or at the end of a text*

18 *Peter Parler's design for a window*

17 18

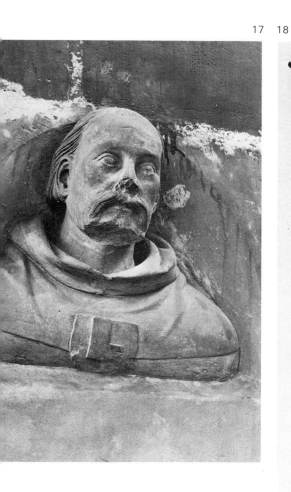

Auid en ainsi de quan
tes uertus et de quantz
biens il a este aucteur
a ceulx de sa lignee. et
combien plain de grant aige il est
mort nous lauons declaire ou li

mre deuant dit. Quand salomo
son fil: ancores iceune enfant eut
prins le royaume de son pere. et fu
assis ou siege royal. tout le peuple
solennelment fu seur. comme on
seult faire a un roy au commence

19 *Building the Temple of Solomon. This fifteenth-century illuminated manuscript of Josephus shows a splendid disregard for chronology with its Gothic building and contemporary dress*

20 *Madonna and Child in Cologne Cathedral, carved in wood in about 1320. It is painted, and highly unrealistic in style. The crowns, sceptre and wreath of stars are later, Baroque, additions. The statue is 7 ft. high*

22

23

21 *Illustration from a thirteenth-century French Old Testament showing the great hoist, forerunner of the crane*

22 *Fifteenth-century manuscript showing the simultaneous construction of twelve churches in fulfilment of a vow. They were in fact built consecutively but here the artist has shown in one picture the various stages of construction*

23 *Anne, Duchess of Bedford, kneeling before St Anne. Bedford Book of Hours*

24a

b

c

d

e

f

g

24 *Seven pictures from an illuminated manuscript:*
(a) *The Sacrifice of Isaac*
(b) *Moses and the Tablets of the Law*
(c) *The Annunciation*
(d) *The Nativity*
(e) *The Flight into Egypt*
(f) *The Miracle at Cana*
(g) *The Crucifixion*

25 *Pilate washing his hands. Eleventh-century fresco in St Angelo in Formis, near Capua*

26 *The Plague Cross, Cologne, fourteenth century. The calm, crowned majesty of the crucified God of earlier centuries has given way to the almost horrific realism of the tortured Man. The classic, geometric serenity of the cross itself has become a twisted tree*

26

27 *Reliquary of the Holy Thorn. Made for the Duke of Orleans, brother of Charles VI, the Thorn is held upright in a huge sapphire, and pearls liberally stud the gold. The figure of Christ, seated on a rainbow with his feet on the Globe, seems cramped and insecure, and the circling crown of saints irrelevant*

28, 29 *The stained glass of Chartres*

28   29

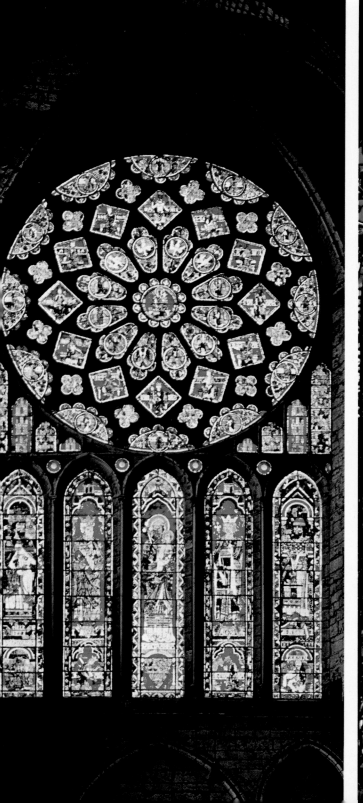

30, 31 *La Sainte Chapelle, Paris. The circle is a recurring symbol in iconography; appearing as a rose window it is the Sun, which is also Christ*

32 *The oxen of Laon. Sixteen life-size stone oxen were hauled to the top of this great tower to stand, in a forest of turrets, peering down in mild bewilderment over Laon*

33 *The Douce Apocalypse, English thirteenth-century manuscript. Superficially it is an idyllic subject but it is couched in the symbolism of St John and is therefore appalling, for the wine is blood.*

'And another angel came out of the temple which is in heaven, he also having a sharp sickle. And another angel came out from the altar, which had power over fire; and cried with a loud cry to him that had the sharp sickle, saying, Thrust in thy sharp sickle, and gather the clusters of the vine of the earth; for her grapes are fully ripe. And the angel thrust in his sickle into the earth, and gathered the vine of the earth, and cast it into the great wine-press of the wrath of God. And the wine-press was trodden without the city, and blood came out of the wine-press, even unto the horse bridles, by the space of a thousand and six hundred furlongs.' (*Revelation 14, 17–20*)

33

34

34 *The Masons' Window, Bourges. Sometimes windows in medieval cathedrals depicted the craftsmen about their trades*

35 *The artist at work. Three of the many stages in the preparation of an illuminated manuscript of the mid-fifteenth century*

chapter 4

THE REV. JOHN INNES M.A.

THE EASTERN ORTHODOX CHURCH

The Christian art of eastern Europe, that part of the Christian communion generally known as Eastern Orthodox, has been greatly influenced by military and political factors since the beginning of Christianity. The Roman Empire was the foundation on which civilization could consolidate itself, providing that its philosophies were not seditious, and in AD 260 Christianity became a 'permitted religion' (*religio licta*). Christianity had for some while flourished outside the Empire and in AD 280, as a result of missionary work in Edessa, the King of Armenia established it as the national religion.

However, all was not to remain favourable to the Christians. From AD 303 to 305 the Emperor Diocletian persecuted them with terrible severity and three years later Maximin tried to re-establish paganism. But the persecution and opposition were to be short-lived, and Galerius on his death-bed in 311 signed an edict of toleration, countersigned by his colleagues, Constantine and Licinius. By the Edict of Milan two years later they exhorted the restoration to the Christians of all their places of worship without demand for payment, and then went even further and wrote letters to Proconsuls like Aulinus in Africa actually ordering that such restorations be made. Yet again Constantine sent money to the Bishop of Carthage to assist with the expenses of the clergy and a further letter to Aulinus exempting the clergy from public duties. Finally the wheel turned full circle with an edict forbidding proselytizing by soothsayers: a soothsayer who disobeyed was to be burnt and an informer against a soothsayer merited a reward.

One gets some idea of the Emperor's underlying motive in all these decrees from the writings of the time.

'So that the God who dwells in heaven might be propitious to us and to all under our rule' (Edict of Milan).

'When religion is set at nought, in which is preserved the crowning reverence for the most holy celestial Being, great dangers are brought upon public affairs; but that when legally adopted and safeguarded, it affords to the Roman name the greatest prosperity and exceptional felicity to the affairs of all mankind' (Constantine to Aulinus).

Constantine also shifted his capital to Constantinople,

alternatively known as Byzantium or New Rome, thereby creating a predominantly eastern empire, and as a result many outstanding examples of early Christian art in the West are Byzantine in style. Thus when Constantine died the position of the Church had changed radically, not just locally as in Armenia, but over most of the area through which it had spread. Christians began to think of the Roman Empire as 'Christendom'—a part of the world which had been won for the Christian faith.

But one of the terrible defects of the new situation was that if someone differed from the interpretation of the Christian faith at the centre, then he was thought of not only as being heretical but also as subversive. This helps to explain the severity with which Arian Emperors like Constantius and Orthodox Emperors like Justinian treated their doctrinal opponents.

The word 'Catholic' (from the Greek *catholicos* meaning universal) came to be used of those who held the doctrine of the Trinity, but originally there was no contradiction between the words catholic and orthodox, as this quotation from a decree of the Emperor Theodosius shows:

> They [the heretics] shall be expelled outside the walls of the cities so that the Catholic Churches throughout the world may be restored to the Orthodox bishops who hold the faith of Nicaea.

By the Council of Chalcedon in AD 451 the Church inside the Roman Empire was organized on the basis of one Patriarch in the West, Rome, and four Patriarchs in the East, Constantinople, Alexandria, Antioch and Jerusalem, whose jurisdictions in general corresponded with the races of the Empire, and the term 'orthodox' meaning 'right praise' was used to distinguish the Eastern Church from those churches (mostly beyond the boundaries of the Empire) which refused to accept the definitions of the Council of Chalcedon.

The sack of Rome by the Huns and Goths caused a partial eclipse of Western civilization, but the Church continued its existence and in time began to convert its conquerors. The reconquest of the West some fifty years later by the Byzantine Emperor Justinian initiated new building such as the Church of San Vitale.

Meanwhile the rise of Islam in the desert was to have a profound effect on Christianity. By the end of the eighth century the patriarchates of Alexandria, Antioch and Jerusalem had been overrun and the inhabitants given the simple choice between Allah and the sword. However, the Church was not stagnant and a steady missionary effort resulted in the conversion to Christianity of Bulgaria and western Russia by the end of the tenth century. The missionary technique was simply to convert the ruler of a territory and thus through his authority

extend Christianity over a wide area. Further, this conversion of rulers encouraged royal patronage of the Church and led to the building of fine basilicas and churches, a practice which the rulers' wealthy subjects like to copy whenever possible.

But the tension which had existed between East and West since Chalcedon mounted steadily, fanned by political, theological and personal rivalry between the Patriarchs in Rome and Constantinople, the only Eastern patriarchate which had not fallen to Islam. In 1054 came the Great Schism. Pope and Eastern Patriarch excommunicated each other and the Christian Church found itself split asunder in a rift that remained unbridged until very recently. The effect on the artistic development of the Eastern Church was to be tremendous.

Scarcely had the ink dried on the Papal Bull of Excommunication before the Catholic Powers embarked on the First Crusade to the Holy Land. Supposedly Christian in concept, led by a military saint, the Crusaders based themselves in Eastern Christendom and set about despoiling the 'heretics' with as much enthusiasm and savagery as they attacked the infidel. The resulting bitterness was not quickly dispelled. Two centuries later the eastern borders of Christendom were devastated by the Tartar invasions of Russia in 1237 and 1242 and the countryside remained as a Tartar province for well over a hundred years. Meanwhile the Turks advanced steadily through the Balkans. In 1453 Constantinople fell and it was not for another century that the Islamic advance was finally halted at the gates of Vienna and Lepanto. Their dominion over the Balkans was to last five hundred years.

Thus there are two great sources of Orthodox artistry; Byzantium from 311 to 1453 and Russia from 1380 to 1917. It is mainly from these two cultures, based on the same theology, that the illustrations are drawn. The October Revolution of 1917 marks the end of an era as definitely as did the Tartar invasion and the fall of Constantinople. A persecution perhaps less brutal but certainly nearly as effective as Diocletian's took place in Russia and spread outwards in the years after 1945. Its subsequent reversal has been purely for political reasons, but it is inevitable that great cathedrals are not built in times of persecution, and the art of the Eastern Orthodox Church is deeply bound up with politics and warfare.

It was quite early in the history of the Eastern Orthodox Church that the question of the theology of art arose. From the earliest period of the Church there were those who thought that art fostered idolatry. The Puritanism of some of the hermits gave no place to Christian art, and under pressure from the challenge of Islam, with its prohibition of representative art, there was a period during which the Emperor actually banned the representative art of the icon. But after a number of battles,

verbal, written and even physical, icons were reinstated by a council of the Church. One of the chief protagonists of Christian art was John of Damascus who wrote from the relative security of a Christian monastery in an Arab-dominated area.

The result of this conflict was a most carefully worked out theology of art. Roughly speaking the defenders of Christian art said that Christ in his human aspect was physical and that there could be no great sin in depicting Him in materials. Furthermore the Gospels contained portraits in words and since Christians did not make mental idols of these no more need they make actual idols of pictures. Admittedly Moses had been forbidden to bow down and worship before idols but he had also been instructed to take wood and carve cherubim for the Ark of the Lord. Accordingly worldly materials could be used to represent spiritual values, but as a safeguard such representation must not too closely resemble the natural objects. Statues, or indeed any figure in the round, were forbidden, nor was an artist encouraged to depict the actual features of his model. Rather he was to represent in the material of his choice his understanding of the spiritual world. An attempt was made to safeguard against a too individual interpretation by very strict rules on how Christ, the Virgin Mary and the Apostles and saints should be drawn and on how certain scenes should be portrayed. Thus a thirteenth-century fresco in Serbia and an eighteenth-century icon from the Balkans on the Dormition of Mary will be similar in general outline despite the difference in place, period and material.

Some Orthodox scholars say that you can tell the spiritual depth of the icon painter by his icons; certainly many regard their work as prayer or meditation transposed into art. This attitude resembles modern art in one respect in that the artist does not want to copy or 'photograph' the natural world even when his technical ability would enable him so to do; on the contrary he is anxious to avoid this. There however the similarity ceases; the modern artist expresses what *he* wants to say from his own intellect and imagination; the icon painter is concerned to express the faith of the Church, permitting his inspiration to expound its truths.

Among the illustrations are a few from Armenia. The Armenian Church is one of the Ancient Apostolic Churches of the East (Syrian Orthodox, Assyrian, etc.) which lay beyond the boundaries of the Roman Empire and refused to accept the findings of the Council of Chalcedon. Possibly as a legacy from the iconoclastic controversy or possibly because of the proximity of the Moslem cultures of the Turkish and Persian Empires, the Armenians generally avoided representational art in the churches, but like the Moslems (and to some extent the Celts) used mainly patterns and floral designs.

The content of the faith as well as the practice of the Orthodox Churches acted not only as an inspiration but also as a severe limitation on the artist. In the sixteenth century the 'tent' style of building had been developed, based on the application to stone building of the designs of wooden churches in northern Russia, the classic prototype being the church in the village of Kolomenskoye, but when the Patriarch Nikhon wanted to bring the nationalistic Russian Church more into line with contemporary Orthodox practice he forbade this style of architecture and insisted on a reversion to the traditional Greek style of a church with a single or five domes, and 'tent' design is thereafter found only in belfries.

Carving on the outside of churches was occasionally permitted though it was rare after the thirteenth century and statues continued to be forbidden. In the secular atmosphere of the eighteenth century this rule was sometimes broken in a desire to emulate Western practice, as in the Dubrovtsi church in Moscow. But the artist who was an innovator very often took church art away from its theological justification. In the nineteenth century the romantic styles of Western painting affected not only artists of religious subjects like Ivanov but icon painters as well. Sugary and sentimental pictures of Christ and the Virgin Mary appeared. The Russians referred to this as painting 'in the Italian style' but once it had spread to such centres of Orthodoxy as Mount Athos the Greeks described it as painting 'in the Russian manner'!

In the Christian churches of the East the interior was decorated in such a way as to set the stage for the Eucharistic Liturgy. In the fourth or fifth centuries it was usual for a church to be decorated with mosaics or frescoes in set positions, although by the eleventh century these had been moved from the walls to an iconostasis, a screen which divided the sanctuary from the rest of the church. Christ as the ruler of all things (Pantocrater) was set in the dome which represented heaven; below Him angels and sometimes the Twelve Apostles, then the Virgin Mary in the attitude of a Jewish woman at prayer and below that the Communion of the Apostles. On the walls, which represented the means of communication between heaven and earth, between God and man, were depicted scenes from the Gospels or from the lives of the Apostles, saints, martyrs and passion-bearers. The icon of the 'Communion of the Apostles' sometimes copied the actual layout of the Holy Table during a contemporary celebration of the Eucharistic Liturgy and sometimes it represented a tradition of the remote past which was being continued in art long after the practice had been altered. It is probable that in the eleventh century mosaic in St Sophia, Kiev, the instruments of the Liturgy are set out as used in that period.

Other aspects of the Liturgy promoted special forms of art—the vestments worn by the priest, patens, chalices, covers for the service books and the cross with which the priest blessed the people at the end of the service, and the sivot, the casket in which small quantities of consecrated bread, intincted with consecrated wine and then dried, were reserved for the sick. Besides the Eucharistic Liturgy other special services need special liturgical items such as the crowns used during the marriage service and the epitaphion, the cloth on which is embroidered a portrait of the dead Christ, which is carried round the church on Good Friday and laid on a special tomb in the centre of the church.

From the earliest times it was the practice amongst devout Christians to make pilgrimages to holy places, firstly of course to Nazareth, Bethlehem and Jerusalem, then later to places of special virtue such as the monasteries at Mount Athos or Theodosius in Kiev and the burial-places of martyrs and missionaries, St Naum's church on Lake Ohrid. In time, thanks to the donations of pilgrims, these places grew wealthy and became beautifully decorated, but they also suffered from commercial exploitation, one of the more popular souvenirs being a lead phial with an appropriate icon stamped on to its surface, the precursor of the picture postcard and the colour transparency!

But as a national Church tended to develop within the Orthodox Communion so did a national artistic style under the

3

influence of geography and politics. The short-lived 'tent' style and the subsequent onion domes of Russia and the Moravska style of Serbia are developments from the original Byzantine culture. The cross itself underwent varied artistic treatment. Often on church domes the simple cross was elaborated into an upright with three horizontal cross-bars, the uppermost representing the inscription placed by Pilate above the head of Christ and the lowest a cross-member used to support the weight of the crucified body. And as the Muscovites drove the Tartars out of Russia the cross was sometimes shown triumphant above the crescent of Islam. In Central Russia the influence of Persian miniatures can be seen in some of the icons, particularly in the depicting of horses, whilst the compulsory introduction of

4

Western culture by Peter the Great produced in Leningrad a style of church building which is obviously imported.

But whatever its period and whatever the influences from which a work of Christian art is derived the only true yardstick by which it can be measured is whether or not it bears true or false witness to the faith it proclaims. Thus alone can it be judged.

5–8 *The decorations of early churches always explained the liturgical actions which took place in them, as shown in this mosiac floor of AD 320 in a non-Roman centre, Aquelia*

5 *A worshipper deposits a* prosphora *(small loaf) in an offertory basket*

6 *A deacon carries the offertory basket to the place of preparation. His dress is the 'best clothes' of a gentleman of the period and not yet vestments*

7 *The place where the Eucharistic Table stood. The Nike (Victory) Angel holds up the true offering: the palm of martyrdom and the wreath of Eternal Life expressed through the offering of bread and wine in the offertory basket and* skyphus *(damaged) at his feet*

8 *Detail of Nike Angel*

9 *Baptistry of Callisto, eighth century. The figures in this ancient church are obvious precursors of the Gothic ones at Chartres and elsewhere in the West*

10 *The Church of Ivan Krestitel (St John the Baptist); now a sanctuary for precious things found in other churches. The ikon shown is of the fifth century and depicts Empress Helena and Emperor Constantine who were regarded as saints by the Eastern Orthodox Church after the Great Schism*

11, 12 (overleaf) *Christianity did not invent any new kinds of building. The Christians always adapted existing styles of houses, basilicas, temples, for their places of worship, but when they began to decorate them they did so first of all for what went inside rather than for external appearance*

11 *St Sophia, Kiev, 1030–7. Pantocrator. The mosaics are similar to those in Daphne, Greece, of the same period*

12 *Church of the Holy Apostles, Pec, Yugoslavia. Fresco of the Virgin Mary as 'Theotokos' (Godbearer or Mother of God), a title devised to safeguard the divinity of her Son rather than as a personal honour*

10

13, 14 *The buildings became divided by screens. At first these were only waist-high and acted as crush barriers to keep the place of the liturgical action free for movement. Uprights and a beam were added later, and later still even the openings of beams were filled with icons, of which there were sometimes several tiers*

13 *Church of the Prophet Elias*

14 *Lintula Convent, Finland*

13

15 *In the earliest days a great variety of iconography illustrated the meaning of the liturgical action. By the fifth century this had become conventional in arrangement. Later it was concentrated on the iconostasis screen, leaving the walls for the more popular devotion of the saints*

16 (overleaf) *This view of the interior of the Orthodox church at Chevtogne, Belgium, shows the iconography and wall-paintings in their full glory*

15

17 *Detail from the sanctuary at Chevtogne showing SS. Cyril, Gregory and Nicholas*

18 *Sopocani, Serbia, 1263. The back or west wall of the church was originally the place for the Last Judgement. With the concentration of liturgical iconography on the screen it becomes the place for the Dormition of Our Lady*

19–29 *This series of pictures shows the sequence of the Liturgy*

19 *Preparation of the* prosphora *at the Prothesis Table. The ceremonial preparation of the bread and wine has become so complicated that it has been moved to before the service proper. It takes place at a table in an apse to the left of the main sanctuary. Note the design on the bread*

20 *The 'Little Entrance'; the Book of the Gospels is carried in. This was originally the beginning of the Liturgy. Note the magnificent vestments used in quite a poor church in Dalmatia*

21 *Litany. With the gradual closing of the screen by icons it becomes an important function of the deacon to keep the congregation in touch with what is happening at the table. This is done in a series of Litanies, 'Popular Devotions' that have been added to all Orthodox services*

22 *Reading of the Gospel. The lessons are read in a language understood by the people. The mission of Cyril and Methodius to the Slavs made use of the Slavonic language both for the scriptures and all services, and the practice was carried on in Serbia, Russia and Bulgaria*

20

21   22

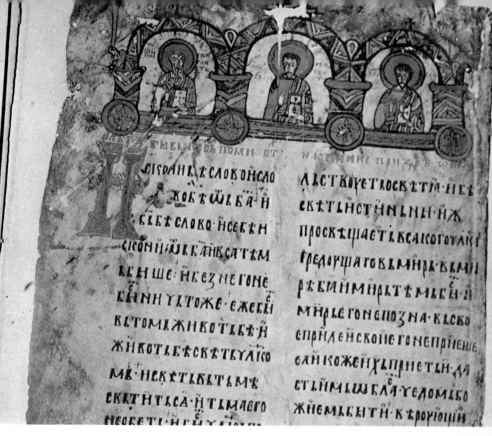

23 *The Great Entrance. Worship on earth is an icon of worship in heaven. Above the altar in the Novodevichi Convent, Moscow, is a magnificent carving of the Six-Winged Seraphim mentioned in the vision of Isaiah*

24 *A Gospel Book from Miroslav*

25 *The Great Entrance is sometimes interpreted as representing the Entry of Christ into Jerusalem. The scene here is shown in inlaid wood in the Novodevichi Convent*

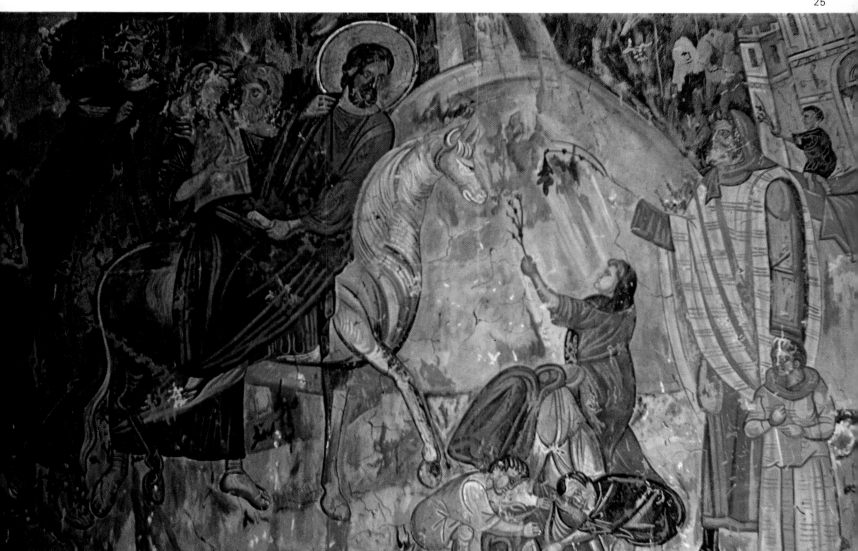

26 *The Great Entrance. The priest carries in the Holy Gifts of bread and wine and the choir sing the 'Cherubic Hymn'*

27 *The Altar or 'Holy Table', as it is called, is free-standing. The priests move round it to receive Communion in two kinds separately. The people receive outside the screen; both kinds are given together in a spoon to the standing communicants*

28 *Elevation. The priest holds up the consecrated elements of bread and wine in a gesture of offering*

29 *The Eucharistic Liturgy ends with the giving out of the 'Antidoron', unconsecrated bread, instead of the Gifts. A scene from the New Valaamo Monastery, Finland, with the original icon of Our Lady of Konevitsa in the background*

30 *The consecrated Gifts are also kept in a 'sivot' for taking Communion to the sick. No ceremonial honour is paid to the Sacrament until preparations are made to give the Communion. This elaborate example in the shape of a Russian church is in the museum of the Monastery of Caves, Kiev*

31 *Sometimes, but not always, a sermon is given. This finely decorated pulpit is in SS. Peter and Paul, Leningrad*

29

30

31

32

32 *One emperor banned representational art. Roof-painting from a rock church at Goreme, Turkey*

33 *Behind and above the Holy Table there is usually a fresco or mosaic of the Communion of the Apostles. Generally Christ is shown twice, on one side holding out the consecrated bread and on the other delivering the consecrated wine in a large skyphus, bowl or chalice. This way of giving Communion was described by St Cyprian in the third century*

33

36

34 *More recently Turkish soldiers have mutilated the faces of frescoes, mosaics and icons. The church in Spocani showing such frescoes despoiled after the Turkish victory at Kossovo*

35 *Court Chapel at Plisca, the first capital of the Bulgars. This church shows an arrangement of the sanctuary which the Syrians had used in the fourth century*

36 *St George, Yuriev Polski, the last stone church built in Russia before the Mongol invasion*

37 *Statue of Vladimir, Grand Duke of Kiev. It stands at Novgorod above the spot where the citizens were baptized in the River Dnieper in AD 988*

38 *Church of the Holy Wisdom, Ohrid. This fresco of Popes was painted in 1042, only twelve years before the excommunications in the name of the Pope of Rome and the Patriarch of Constantinople from which the Great Schism is generally dated*

37   38

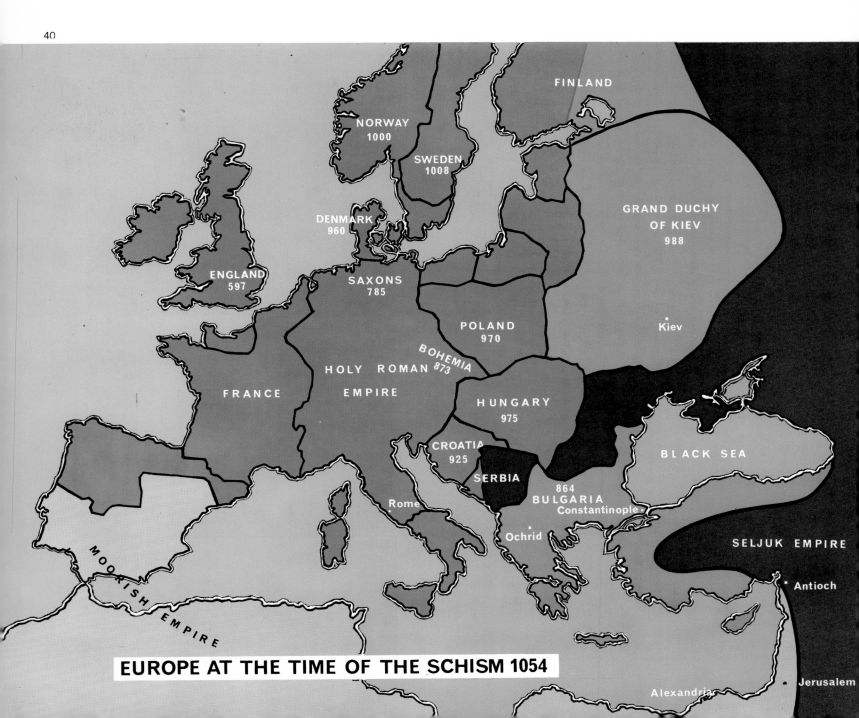

39 *Fortified monastery built in 1418 at Manasija, Serbia*

40 *Map showing the extent of Christianity and its division into Eastern Orthodoxy and Roman Catholicism by the Great Schism of 1054*

41 *Hand-tinted photograph of St Basil's, Moscow, from an album collected by Lady Llangattock during a tour at the end of the nineteenth century*

40

FINLAND

NORWAY
1000

SWEDEN
1008

GRAND DUCHY
OF KIEV
988

DENMARK
960

ENGLAND
597

SAXONS
785

Kiev

POLAND
970

BOHEMIA
873

HOLY ROMAN
EMPIRE

FRANCE

HUNGARY
975

CROATIA
925

BLACK SEA

SERBIA

Rome

864
BULGARIA
Constantinople

Ochrid

MOORISH EMPIRE

SELJUK EMPIRE

Antioch

EUROPE AT THE TIME OF THE SCHISM 1054

Alexandria

Jerusalem

42 *Konevitsa Icon at New Valaamo. The icon was brought from Mount Athos in 1395 to a monastery on an island in Lake Ladoga. Greek and Russian missionaries probed north to Lapland and across the continent to Alaska in the eighteenth century. The icon is protected by a metal and jewelled cover which is swung open on great festivals*

43 *In this icon of SS. Flaurus and Laurus the horses resemble those in some Persian miniatures*

44, 45 *Interior and exterior of St Nicholas, Leningrad, built by Rastrelli 1753–62, showing Russian adaptation of Baroque*

46 *Many of the country houses in the Classical Revival had chapels in a matching style. This church is on the estate at Kusskovo and was owned by the Sheremetiev family*

42   43

46

47 *Type of roof and window decoration typical of the Princedom of Moldavia. Many of these churches are painted outside*

48 *Church of St Lazar, Serbia, illustrating the elaborate carving and patterns sometimes known as Moravian style*

49 *Patriarch Nikhon declared some national architectural tendencies to be heretical, including 'tent-'style churches. This is the church at Zagorsk, built in 1537*

50 *Russian church in the Garden of Gethsemane, Jerusalem*

51 *Carving of St Dmitri Vladimir, 1194–7*

49

47

50

48

5

52 (opposite) *Façade of the Greek Orthodox Church, Jerusalem*

53

53 *Carving from the Church of the Cross (Djvaari) outside Mtskheta, Georgia, AD 619–39*

54 *Icon in St Isaac's, Leningrad, 1817–57*

55 *Crowns used in the marriage service. This example from Taipala, Finland, is several centuries old. The 'Crowns of Life' express the belief that the relationship begun with marriage does not end with death but continues for eternity*

54　55

56 *Fresco on the outside of the painted monastery of Dragomira, Moldavia, which is a calendar of the saints commemorated by the Church. A technique of fresco painting was known in Moldavia which keeps the external paintings glowing with colour*

57

58

57, 58 *After the fall of Constantinople in 1453, Muscovite Russia was the largest state in 'Orthodoxy'. As it began to win back lands from the Tartars, now Moslem, the Cross was placed above the Crescent. 57, Novodevichy Belfry, Moscow, 58, Donskoi Monastery, Moscow*

59 *The Monastery of the Trinity and St Sergius, Zagorsk, a place of pilgrimage for many centuries*

60 *The Monastery of the Caves, Kiev*

59

60

chapter 5

THE REV. J. HOLLAND-SMITH M.A.

ROME AND THE RENAISSANCE

The Renaissance, which reached its maturity in Italy in the fifteenth and sixteenth centuries, was the fruit of a thirteenth-century marriage between Judae-Arabic learning and Romance intellectual curiosity.

During the early Christian centuries, any creation of the Hellenistic and Roman pagan world which had not been 'baptized' as it were by the early Fathers was condemned as an invention of the Devil for the seduction of the minds and souls of men. Classical paintings and sculpture were covered up and destroyed. Classical books were banned, defaced for the use of their precious parchment in palimpsests or actually burned, and classical thought was more or less deliberately suppressed. Generalizing, we might say that traditional Christian learning petrified in the West in the years between the death of Augustine of Hippo (AD 430) and the election of Gregory I (AD 590). By the eleventh century, classical mythology and philosophy were scarcely more than a memory in western Europe—and that memory was more likely to provoke a shudder than stimulate a mind to wonder. A barbarous Greek was still spoken in Apulia and Calabria, but elsewhere the very language of the Gospels was forgotten. Increasingly, Canon Law occupied the attention of ambitious Churchmen.

Gradually, however, Europe awakened from the darkness of the centuries of the barbarian invasions. Christian victories in the Spanish peninsula, southern Italy and the Holy Land itself brought first Christian merchants and pilgrims and then Christian scholars into touch with Arab and Jewish thinkers among whom the memory—and the texts—of the greatest minds of Greece had been kept alive. Byzantine art began to be known, if not yet appreciated except as a curiosity, through Norman conquests in southern Italy and Greece, and the contacts of the Crusaders with the Byzantines—contacts culminating, to the shame of the West, in the sack of Constantinople in 1204.

The first light of the new dawn showed in the far West as early as the eleventh century, when Anselm of Canterbury wrote his *Cur Deus Homo?* in which he brought logic to the aid of apologetics. A generation or so later, Hugh of St Victor's (*d.* 1141) taught that God was to be served through the free choice of man's free spirit, and could be found through reason and understanding as well as faith and love. Alain de Lille (*d*. 1202) took these new developments in Western thinking a revolutionary stage further by attempting a reasoned synthesis of the ascetic Christianity current in his own day, by which 'the word' was despised, with a positive assessment of the natural creation: arguing that the cosmos was good, like the God who created it, he pleaded that nature should be left free, so that natural development could bring into being a new man, 'the Youth', who unlike the men of his own day would live in harmony with the whole universe.

So unprecedented a reappraisal of the part of nature in the Divine plan was possible only in the light of a great labour of translation which had been undertaken in Europe during the previous half-century. The first steps towards the rediscovery of philosophy had been taken at Toledo, where Archbishop Raymond I, recognizing the value of Aristotelean method for teaching logic—a science his clergy needed in their debate with the surviving Arabs of the Spanish peninsula—had founded a school of translation. The Toledo school translated the whole corpus of Aristotelean works preserved in Arabic into Latin. The texts were of uneven quality. Many of the works were Neoplatonist rather than Aristotelean. But their valuable insights far outweighed their shortcomings. Aristotle and his followers revealed to Alain of Lille and his contemporaries the order underlying and sustaining visible phenomena—a reasonable world, in which effects followed causes, and words could be found to describe and explain the relations between them. Once the minds of men had been given a glimpse of this new world of thought, there was no turning them back. At Chartres, even the Koran was studied together with the Neoplatonist teachings of such unorthodox Moslems as Al-kindi, Avicenna and Averroes (*d*. 1198). In the thirteenth century the new learning gave rise to new schools of 'progressive, liberal' Christian philosophy, first at the University of Paris (founded in 1205), then at other centres of learning in the West. To conservative, ascetic scholars these new schools seemed likely to overthrow the whole Christian religion and with it the edifice of Western society. Aristotelean method and doctrines were condemned by Pope Innocent III in 1210, and again by Gregory IX twenty years later, although in those twenty years the situation had so far changed that Gregory's condemnation was to operate only until the texts were corrected. Soon, Aristoteleanism became the dominant form and method of Christian philosophy. In the great syntheses of Albertus Magnus, St Bonaventure and St Thomas Aquinas (*d*. 1274) it gave a respectable philosophical framework to the history of salvation. Fundamental to all Aquinas's thinking was the thesis that the first victim of sin was human reason: 'the firstborn daughter of iniquity', he wrote, 'is blindness of the intellect'. The sinful man is therefore un-

reasonable: the holy are reasonable, and their reason brings them to God.

In the hierarchy of the physical senses, Aquinas put sight above the rest. It seemed to him that clarity of vision, both physical and mental, would lead to spiritual perspicacity and thus to the ultimate good, the vision of God.

It also led to a new vision of the world, and was ultimately one of the sources both of the Renaissance in art and of the Reformation in religion.

Extreme Aristoteleanism never won a complete victory. Aquinas himself was convinced that it should not be permitted to do so. During his lifetime he was accused by ultra-Aristoteleans of mysticism and by ultra-conservatives of atheism. But when he died, 'thomism', as his form of synthetic Catholic Aristoteleanism later came to be called, was already firmly rooted: within forty years, it was to be the only respectable Catholic philosophy.

It was the curiosity about the world which the new scholarship encouraged that opened the way to the development of Renaissance art. The Byzantine vision of sanctity, the devotion of Peter Abelard and his followers to the Magdalene as the most human of saints, and the love of Creation evinced by St Thomas are all combined in the work of the first painters known to us who unmistakably belonged to the Renaissance: Duccio of Siena who began to paint in 1279, only five years after Thomas's death; Simone Martini, also of Siena, and the Florentines Cimabue and Giotto, who began work on the frescoes of the Life of St Francis at Assisi in the year 1290. The influence of the Byzantine painters of heaven is especially obvious in the work of the Sienese school: Florentine figures and settings were more natural from the first. But in both Siena and Florence the new vision of the world had already brought new life to painting.

The new way of looking at the world brought rapid changes, not only to religion and painting, but also to architecture, literature and even political theory. (The name of Dante stands supreme in the fourteenth century: he was a Catholic Christian, although like most of the new men, he was often in conflict with the authorities of the Church.) At Florence, Giotto was followed by a host of pupils and imitators, among whom Daddi and Orcagna were outstanding; Siena continued to be strongly influenced by the mysticism of the Byzantines and late medieval 'conservatives'. Neither Simone Martini nor his contemporaries Pietro and Ambrogio Lorenzetti quite succeeded in anchoring their figures to earth—and may well not have intended to do so. Their saints and angels do not belong to earth. They use it as a stage on which to play out the drama of heaven and redemption, with everyday terrestrial objects as their stage properties.

It was only at the close of the fourteenth century that the
new vision gave birth to significantly non-medieval sculpture,
in the work of Jacopo della Quercia at Bologna and elsewhere,
and outside Italy in the experiments of Claus Sluter of Haar-
lem, an older contemporary of the Van Eyck brothers.

Already before this, however, those who had learned to
express the spirit of the age in paint were learning to do so in
solid form, in architecture. The cathedral of Florence is the
best known of these new creations. It was designed at the end of
the thirteenth century by Arnolfo di Cambio on French (Gothic)
models, but after his death the work was entrusted in turn to
Giotto, Pisano and Talenti, then to a committee of architects,
sculptors, and painters. Giotto concentrated on the campanile,
the earliest and most 'Gothic' of all Renaissance ecclesiastical
buildings in Florence. Although it was still 'Gothic'—a term
invented by the Florentines in disparagement of the allegedly
uncouth work of earlier centuries—it had little in common with
French and English designs of the same period (*c.* 1344). Its
unique character saved it when the façade of the cathedral,
built by Talenti later in the century, was torn down at the
beginning of the next to make way for true Renaissance work.

For the Catholic Church in the West, the late fourteenth and

early fifteenth centuries were a time of confusion and often near-despair. The Avignon Captivity (1310–74), during which the popes lived in France under the direction of French kings, was followed almost immediately by the Great Schism of the West (1378–1415), during which at one moment three popes claimed to rule the Church. Heresy was preached in England by Wycliffe and in Bohemia by Hus. Nationalism was a growing and dividing force. Using the methods of Aquinas and later teachers of the Canon Law, and making full use of their new knowledge of the history of institutions and ideas, teachers both orthodox and semi-orthodox began to debate the true nature of the authority of the popes. The Councils of Constance (1415–17) and Pavia-Siena (1423), where papal rule was challenged, and of Florence (1439), which had temporary success in uniting the Eastern and Western Churches, were as valid expressions of the new age as the autocratic rule of the Medici in Florence or the Visconti in Milan. They expressed the new individualism in collectivity, just as kings and princes were expressing it in autocracy and semi-overt independence from the popes—and painters and sculptors were expressing it in artistic originality.

And what great artists they were! Ghiberti, Donatello, Fra Angelico, Uccello, della Robbia, Masaccio, Fra Filippo Lippi: all these giants and many lesser men were already working in Florence before the birth of Botticelli (1444) or Leonardo da Vinci (1452) and the fall of Constantinople (1453). In this first half of the fifteenth century the movement born in Tuscany spread to Umbria—where the greatest names were da Fabriano, Pisano and Piero della Francesca—and to Padua. Soon it was to embrace all northern Italy, carrying with it everywhere a love of light and life as the creation of God.

Although many of the works of the Cinquecento were religious, not all of them were. Portraiture was of growing importance, and the recognition of the devotion to life shewn by the artists and writers of the pre-Christian classical world was leading to a revival of interest in classical subjects drawn from mythology and allegory—an interest further stimulated by the revival of Greek studies at the universities and the sudden availability of Greek manuscripts following the dispersal of the libraries of Constantinople. Religious asceticism was no longer permitted to dominate the artist—and if this was a good thing, the Medici princes deserve much of the credit for it. It is more than the technical improvement of a hundred years of artistic development that distinguishes, for instance, Ghiberti's panel 'The Creation of Eve' from the second bronze door of the Baptistry at Florence (1425–52) from Andrea Pisano's sculpture of the same scene on the campanile (c. 1340). Not only is Ghiberti's Eve more sensual, his God the Creator more majestic, his Adam more naturally asleep: there is breathable air between

them. God, man and the world are all more 'real'. Gothic asceticism and mysticism have become wholly alien. In a few years' time, Botticelli will be able to paint 'The Birth of Venus' and the even more earthly 'Primavera'—and still be called to Rome to work for the Pope.

In fact, art and religion were drifting apart. Although the masters of the next hundred years—Andrea Mantegna, Leonardo, Michelangelo and Raphael—worked frequently and brilliantly under ecclesiastical patronage, a later generation judged them and their contemporaries to have all but destroyed the Church. The dream of making Rome the centre of the new art and culture was Pope Nicholas V's (1447–55). It was he who called for plans for a new St Peter's and founded the Vatican Library. His successors followed his lead. The new art flourished in Rome—and so also, men said, did the 'new' pagan vices. The judgement of Adrian VI at his election in 1522 was that under the influence of artists who were neo-pagans and the direction of popes who were the kinsmen of poisoners 'the Roman Church has been the primary source of all the evils which good men everywhere are lamenting'. His view was endorsed by the new reformers; Luther, who had nailed the Ninety-Five Theses against indulgences to the door of the church at Wittenberg four years earlier, Calvin and the Protestants of the north.

Whether, however, these artists worked for art's sake or for God's sake, the Church had reason—and has reason—to be grateful to them. They were intensely self-conscious men, working not—as the medieval painters had done—primarily to illustrate themes, but to re-create a world and people it. 'If a painter yearns for fair women to kindle his love,' Leonardo wrote, 'he has the power to create them, and if he wants to see monsters to arouse his fear, his amusement and laughter, or even his compassion—he is their Lord and Creator.' For the Faithful, he created above all a new image of the Holy Family, a family so human that it reveals its links with divinity through its very humanity. His 'Virgin and Child with St Anne' (c. 1500) or his cartoon of the Head of Christ need no identifying labels to make them significant . . . but the same might be said of his 'Bacchus'—which has actually sometimes been identified as St John the Baptist. His contemporary, Raphael, although technically so assured, sometimes slipped over the edge from dignity into sentimentality—a pitfall ever afterwards gaping for Italian Catholic painters—and in punishment, as it were, his saints wear aureoles to mark them off from more earthy sitters.

The Church was poised for collapse when Michelangelo Buonarroti was commissioned in 1508 by Julius II, della Rovere, to decorate the ceiling of the Sistine Chapel: when thirty years later he painted the Last Judgement behind the

altar, the flood of the Protestant Reformation had washed up to the very frontiers of Italy. Michelangelo, however, continued in both paint and stone to express the highest aspirations of the Catholic Renaissance, not so much the destruction of the old world as the synthesis between the Creator and his creation, between heaven and earth. Artistically, his concern was almost solely with the perfect representation of the male figure—the whole world knows 'David', 'Moses' and the 'Christ' of the Vatican 'Pietà'—but philosophically and spiritually he gave expression to all that the earliest orthodox Catholic painters of the Renaissance had been trying to say.

Form—delineated by painters and explored by sculptors—dominated Florentine art and the new Rome of the decadent popes. In the Venice of the Doges, colour, and soon light itself, brought a new dimension to the service of art: Titian, Tintoretto and Veronese all stretched themselves to their artistic limits to reproduce both the grandeur and the atmosphere of Venice, whether their chosen subject was Venice itself or not. Although such work is rarely spiritual—even Titian's 'Burial of Christ' at the Louvre is far more concerned with men in this world than with religion—it rarely falls short of magnificence. It is great art, but few Christians today think of it when they think of religious art. The sixteenth century was characterized by grand emotions, by cruelty, pomp and ceremony. Religion was either intensely private, or intensely public. Private religion produces little art with universal or lasting appeal. Public religion in late sixteenth-century Italy produced such pictures as Veronese's four 'Suppers', painted for the refectories of four monasteries in Venice, and although allegedly illustrating Gospel themes, were set not in occupied Palestine but in aristocratic Italy. This failure in mood—if 'failure' is not too strong a word for what are, after all, artistically speaking, magnificent works—was a typical shortcoming of the painters of the period. In it, as well as in their handling of light and shade for effect, they were reflecting the Catholic and Italian defiant assertiveness which was one of the sources of the Baroque. After them, unfortunately, the road led generally downwards, although individual artists still proved strong-willed enough to leave the road and beat their own paths to the heights.

Baroque painting, sculpture and architecture was the art characteristic of the Catholic countries in the seventeenth and eighteenth centuries. It was the art of the Counter-Reformation, and in Germany, of the period of reconstruction after the Thirty Years War. Its first exponent—so powerful a painter that many do not number him among the artists of the Baroque—was the second Michelangelo, da Caravaggio, a swashbuckling figure in life as in art, often in prison and often in the courts of princes.

It is significant that two of his finest works were commissioned by the most reactionary of all Catholic institutions, the Sovereign and Military Order of St John of Malta.

Dramatic poses, dramatic lighting, the violent expression of truth—so violent as sometimes and increasingly to slip over the edge into rhetoric—marked the art as surely as they marked the arguments of the Counter-Reformation. El Greco's work in Spain, the home of the new Jesuit Order, reflected the same concern with aggressive statement. His style has been described as a mixture of ice and fire. Unfortunately in his religious work he sometimes slipped into producing a blend of sugar and salt. Later in Spain, as elsewhere in Catholic Europe, the salt lost its savour, and damp sugar was all that was left. By the time of Murillo (d. 1682), melancholy charm had swallowed both devotion and realism.

Meanwhile in Italy, too, the genius of painters seemed spent. The great builders were the new force, mightiest of them all, Lorenzo Bernini and his contemporaries in Rome. At the beginning of the sixteenth century, Michelangelo had been commissioned to decorate the Sistine Chapel, but had dominated it in the end. The Baroque artists were true decorators—although brilliant ones. They took themselves seriously enough, but it is often difficult for us to take them seriously. They were greatly influenced by the theatre, the dominant art of their time. Despite the fact that neither their taste nor that of their patrons was sure, however, a kind of perfection is to be seen in, for example, the Cornaro Chapel in Santa Maria della Vittora at Rome, or, in a different and later vein, the churches of Catholic Bavaria. Typically, their general design is more important than any individual part of them. The whole work, floor to roof, door to high altar, is planned to make an impact. The Baroque soon degenerated into Rococo as the Counter-Reformation degenerated into quietism on the one hand and romantic aristocratic 'isolationism' on the other: a spirit most magnificently expressed in the delicate work of the eighteenth-century Tiepolo. By then, the torch lit by Giotto's master Cimabue had passed into other hands, the hands of the Flemish, Dutch and English painters, whose master was that energetic painter of the generous flesh of Flanders, Peter Paul Rubens. Himself a Catholic, he sometimes painted for ecclesiastical patrons. But it is difficult to find even in such works as his declaredly Christian 'Holy Family' in the Wallace Collection or his 'Triumph of the Church' worked in tapestry by the de Vos as vivid a realization of the spiritual reality underlying the flesh as in the Neoplatonist secular portraits of Leonardo, or even of Titian.

Of those lesser men whose sugary sentimentality or grandiose failure seduced Catholic minds between the early seventeenth

5 BERNARDO DADDI: The Nativity. *Daddi was the most 'primitive' of all the Renaissance painters. Yet his Madonna and angels (or are they shepherds?) are more human than any Byzantine figures, and their poses set them firmly in this world*

6 PIETRO LORENZETTI: The Madonna and Child with St John The Evangelist and St Francis. *Assisi. The Basilica of St Francis, Lower Church. The figures are posed against the background, but are free from it*

century and the beginning of the modern movement in art, the less said the better. The most valuable artists of these decades were those less assuming men who were content to be illustrators: men who having learned their trade and the techniques of the Renaissance masters as far as they were able to absorb them, produced illustrations of themes, in the spirit of the despised Gothic (although not in its forms), suitable for the decoration of churches, to remind men of God.

6

7 — 7 LORENZO GHIBERTI: The Creation of Adam and Eve. *Florence. Baptistry, second Bronze Door*

8 JACOPO DELLA QUERCIA: The Creation of Adam. *Bologna. Church of San Petronio. Della Quercia's first concern in this carving was not with grace but with power. His God-the-Creator could have been carved in an earlier period, but this Adam is a figure of the new age*

9 ANDREA PISANO: The Creation of Eve. *Florence. Giotto's Tower. Comparison of these two realizations of the same subject, separated by just a century, vividly demonstrates how far Florentine taste had changed in that time. The movement was even more rapid than that which had transformed Greek art two thousand years earlier and took place in much the same direction*

10 MASACCIO: The Most Holy Trinity. *Florence. Church of Santa Maria Novella. Discoveries in the science of optics made possible Masaccio's application of perspective and generous use of space to give nobility to his painting*

8

9

11 SPAGNA: The Annunciation. *Assisi. S. Maria degli Angeli, Porziuncola Chapel. The realism of the figure is far removed from the formal delineation of Lorenzetti and Daddi*

12 PIERO DELLA FRANCESCA: The Nativity. *Cool, deliberate, classic in a way that other painters of his century often tried to be and failed, della Francesca gives us in this picture a Child to worship and a Mother to lead our prayers. There is no mythology here, yet everything has a mythic quality, from the ass singing with the worshipping shepherds-angels to the magpie on the roof of the unlikely ruin forming the byre*

12

13 FILIPPINO LIPPI: The Virgin appearing to St Bernard. *Florence. The Badia Church. Filippino Lippi was the son of another Florentine painter, Lippo Lippi, and the pupil of a third, Botticelli. He was only twenty-three or four when he painted St Bernard's vision for the Badia Church*

14 BOTTICELLI: The Virgin and Child with Six Saints. *Botticelli painted the Madonna and the Holy Child with SS. Catherine, Augustine, Barnabas, John the Baptist, Ignatius and Michael about the year 1487. Melancholy touches all these figures and Botticelli himself was soon to become a follower of the puritanical Savonarola. Although he has been accused of Gothic tendencies, his art and his life both make him a man of his time, torn between neo-classical paganism and traditional Christian asceticism*

14

5

15 DONATELLO: Marble Choir

16 LUCA DELLA ROBBIA: Marble Choir. *Delight in life is the keynote of both these works; that delight which was the mark of early fifteenth-century Florence. Della Robbia's 'Choir' was inspired by Psalm 150*

17 PERUGINO: The Transfiguration. *In the Exchange at Perugia, Perugino brought together the classical and Christian worlds*

6

18 MICHELANGELO BUONARROTI: St Paul. *Siena Cathedral, the Piccolomini Altar. The most obvious feature of this St Paul is its intense Hellenistic humanity. Though the drapery, hair and beard are not natural, the whole figure is so charged with life that it has been said to be a self-portrait of the twenty-seven-year-old Michelangelo*

19 MICHELANGELO BUONARROTI: Pietà. *Florence. The Cathedral. Michelangelo said that the work of the sculptor was to free the statue from the stone entombing it. The Duomo Pietà is unfinished; the life of the stone is not wholly set free. But here is power in death expressed through the complete mastery of the artist over his material, the masterpiece of an ageing genius still learning from his own genius*

20 LEONARDO DA VINCI: Head of the Saviour *(drawing). Romantic? Or Realistic? How else could you draw a dead face that is to come alive again? Leonardo was fired by both scientific curiosity and the romanticism of the mystic; in so many ways he was the embodiment of 'the Youth' that Alain de Lille had written of three centuries earlier. Not himself intensely religious, he yet succeeded in making statements about religion—such as this head—of an inimitable profundity*

18

19

21 LEONARDO DA VINCI: The Virgin and Child with St Anne

22 LEONARDO DA VINCI: Bacchus

23 LEONARDO DA VINCI: St John the Baptist. *A long, thin symbolic cross and a finger pointing heavenward are all that make this a 'Christian' picture, otherwise it would only be the portrait of an effeminate boy*

24

25 (opposite) RAPHAEL: Madonna with a Fish. *To many, Raphael's Madonnas are the peak not only of Italian but of all Christian art*

26 TITIAN: The Burial of Christ. *Light was always the primary concern of the Venetian masters; here darkness, the absence of light, skilfully employed, gives depth to the distress of the mourners and majesty to their dead Master*

27 TINTORETTO: The Glory of Paradise. *'I pray that God'*, *Tintoretto said when the Venetian Senate proposed to offer this commission to Veronese instead of to himself, 'will grant me Paradise in this world, being full of hope that by his grace I shall also have it in the next'*

26

27

28 VERONESE: The Supper at the House of Simon the Pharisee. *One of four Gospel 'Suppers' painted by Veronese, this one was meant to hang in the refectory of the Dominican house of San Zanipolo at Venice. Palestine has been moved to Venice and Simon the Pharisee has become wealthy as a prince*

29 (overleaf) CARAVAGGIO: The Supper at Emmaus. *Caravaggio's masters were themselves trained in the Venetian Schools; colour, light and shade dominated their artistic lives as the fact of the Reformation dominated their religion*

28

30 (preceding page) LORENZO BERNINI: The Ecstasy of St Theresa. *Rome. Cornaro Chapel, S. Maria della Vittoria*

31 (preceding page) PETER PAUL RUBENS: The Assumption of the Virgin. *Rubens's interpretation of this theme is filled with the warmth and richess of life but reveals little awareness of the soul. El Greco's Virgins could reach heaven but we may doubt if Rubens's will get there safely.*

32 EL GRECO: Madonna and Child with St Martina and St Agnes. *El Greco painted the soul of Spain; the Spain of St John of the Cross and St Francis Xavier, of the dark night of the soul and the lightning of inspired faith*

33 LE SUEUR: The Death of St Bruno. *Painted for the Carthusians of the Rue d'Enfer in 1645*

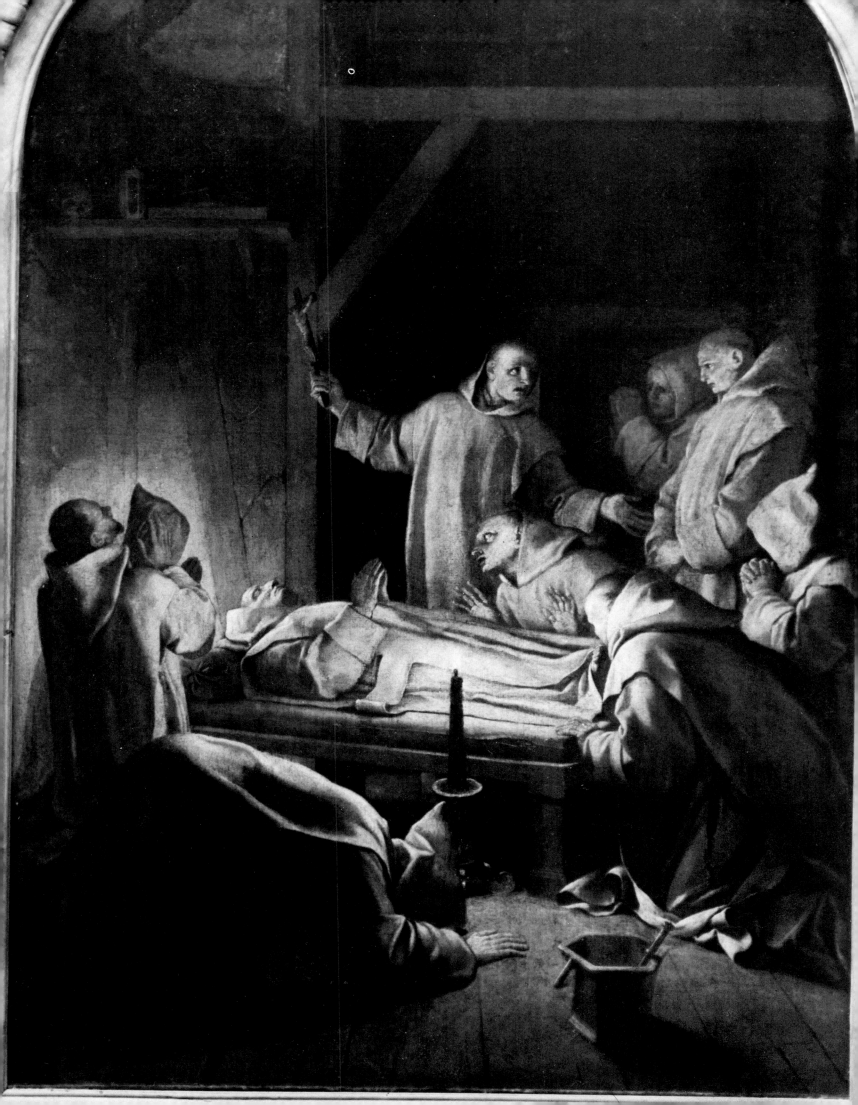

34 PHILIPPE DE CHAMPAIGNE: The Healing of Sister Catherine, Sainte Suzanne on 6 January 1662. *The healing occurred at the end of a novena. The picture records without illuminating the scene or elevating the spectator*

35 JOUVENET: Descent from the Cross. *By the late seventeenth century originality had been lost. Painters like Jouvenet of the French School of Le Brun added nothing to what had been said many times before. Reverent and skilful, all they lacked was the spark of individual genius*

34

36 PEDRO DE MENA: The Virgin of Sorrows. *A dramatic bust in the assertive Baroque style, expressing tragedy, grief and unrelievable melancholy of spirit. The heavy eyebrows, heavy eyelids and sharply defined head-covering extending to the middle of the forehead all heighten the effect*

37 ORTKENS: St John the Baptist Preaching. *The great age of stained glass was the Late Gothic. The discovery of techniques for making large unbroken panes of glass led to a wider use of painting on glass in the period of the Renaissance. It permitted greater detail and realism—but something was lost in freshness of colour and directness of impact*

36

38 GIOVANNI DI STEPHANO: Candlesticks in the Form
of an Angel. *Siena, Duomo. Even the ordinary furniture of
churches was touched by the imagination that fired the High
Renaissance. A candlestick in the form of an angel might
have been produced at any time. But the fine proportions of
these figures, the firmness with which they stand, and the skill
with which they are dressed—to say nothing of the classical
cornucopia which they carry—clearly reveal that their maker
was as aware of the spirit of his times as any of the greater
masters who were his contemporaries*

39 GUGLIELMO DE MARCILLAT:
Adoration of the Magi. *Pope
Leo X, Giovanni de Medici,
commissioned a series of Gospel
scenes from de Marcillat for an
Italian cathedral*

39

ERIC R. DELDERFIELD

There remaineth therefore a rest to the people of God. Heb.IV.9.

ENGLAND AFTER THE REFORMATION

The medieval churches in Britain must indeed have been a riot of colour, beauty and craftsmanship. For centuries men and women had bestowed wealth and love upon them, and, in the thirteenth and fourteenth centuries particularly, there was an intense rivalry between towns and parishes, even between guilds and fraternities. Let a new tower or aisle be added to one church and the zeal of the people of the next parish would know no bounds until they, too, had a similar addition at least as worthy.

The adornment of the churches had, therefore, been a continuous process over the centuries. Until the thirteenth century the faith, piety and generosity of the wealthy had been showered on the religious houses, generally by creating foundations. But gradually these manifestations were directed to other channels. Chief of these was the establishment of chantries, which were a more personal gift and often a form of self-advertisement, for the building of which the services of first-rate craftsmen, often foreigners, were employed. By the commencement of the fourteenth century, this idea had become an expression of the religious life of the times and the churches were considerably enriched thereby.

Inside the church, colour was the dominating feature. Altars gleamed with gold and silver vessels. Many reredoses were works of art. There were magnificent roods and screens, whether of stone or wood did not really matter for both were beautifully painted and gilded. The finest craftsmen contributed. The wood and stone-carvers, smiths for the ironwork, enamellers, goldsmiths, embroiderers, artists and many other specialists vied with each other to produce their best work. There were hangings and decorations at every turn. Wall-paintings were self-explanatory, had no need of words or indeed education to be understood and were immensely popular.

This was a period when men and women lived in a world of fear. They lived close to death and suffering, so that naturally they relied on the comfort that religion could and did bring them. The Church deserved only the best, for did it not by its ritual and pageantry brighten the lives of the common people?

The religious Orders had also become immensely powerful and wealthy, and at the dawn of the sixteenth century the

Church and the religious Orders possessed a fifth of the whole country.

The Reformation in the sixteenth century was dominated by a positive aim. It was the fundamental conviction of the leaders, many of whom were from an educated class which had sprung up among the laity, that the Church of the apostolic age should be recalled and cleansed from medieval corruptions.

Thus, the Reformation was a revival of religion on a grand scale. It would be wrong, however, to dismiss the matter so easily, for the movement was inspired and supported by a number of other forces.

A major factor was the impulse given by the renaissance of learning, which revived the study of ancient civilization. It also emphasized the first pure form of Christianity as represented by the New Testament, a need accentuated by the prevailing impatience with the state of religion in the Church. The scandals of the Papal Court, the narrow life and outlook of the average monk or nun, and the ignorance of many parish clergy, all forced men to re-examine the organization of the Church and contributed to the movement and upsurge that we know as the Reformation. Even the most zealous reformer had no idea of breaking the unity of the Church, and the majority of them held to their Catholicism with fervour.

In Germany, where Luther had kindled the spark of this new thinking in 1517, the struggle ended in 1555 when the signing of the peace of Augsburg formally recognized the Reformed Church as legal. In France the struggle developed into bitter wars and the reformers, at least temporarily, were crushed by the authorities.

In England the course of the Reformation was largely determined by the monarchy and by political considerations and it was not, as was the case almost everywhere else, a popular movement in the true sense of the word. Whilst the impetus of the Reformation can be said to have swept away the monastic establishments, it was the royal supremacy which carried the movement to lengths for which public opinion was then totally unprepared.

The Church and community were probably as close in England as in any other country in the world. Differences between God's law and that of the monarch state were few and a compromise almost always succeeded.

In 1531, owing to political differences, Henry VIII broke with Rome and declared himself head of the Church. The Dissolution of the Monasteries followed five years later. At first only the smaller religious communities, those enjoying an income of less than £200 a year, suffered. Three years later, the legislation extended to the larger monasteries and in a few years more than seven hundred buildings owned by them had to all intents and purposes been obliterated and their immense wealth and possessions confiscated by the Crown. Courtiers crowded in to share the plunder, which was indeed rich.

As far back as 1529, some limitations had been imposed on the chantries, and the monasteries having been effectively dealt with, orders were issued in 1545 under Henry and in 1547, under Edward VI, which unleashed the same ferocity on the chantries.

The edicts gave to the Sovereign all the properties and annuities which had supplied the money to pay the stipends of the chantry priests and, in fact, any funds belonging to the parish guilds and fraternities which could even loosely be said to uphold and perpetuate superstitious objects. Altogether 2,374 guilds and chantries, over a hundred almshouses—or hospitals as they were called—and ninety collegiate foundations were dissolved.

What Henry VIII had started was carried on during the next three reigns. The clergy and churchwardens must have been bewildered by the orders which followed fast upon each other. The reformers held sway during the reign of Edward VI, but much was completely reversed in Mary's brief reign. On Elizabeth's accession yet another reversal and a series of edicts carried on the zealous work begun in her father's reign.

Naturally the altar—the very word denotes sacrifice—felt the full blast of the reformers' zeal and between 1550 and 1564 hundreds of stone altars were smashed. In Elizabeth's reign they were completely forbidden and in their place every church had to be provided with a convenient wooden communion table, which was to be positioned in the centre of the chancel. Certainly the craftsmen in wood came into their own again, for some remarkable examples of rich carving are to be found in these tables today. Those of the Elizabethan period are generally more elaborate, with their superb bulbous legs, whilst the Jacobean pieces are somewhat plainer but nevertheless extremely attractive.

From the earliest days, there had been a division between the altar and the nave, and almost every church had a screen of some kind. These were of stone or wood, depending on the material available locally. They are still comparatively numerous in the counties of Devon, Somerset, Norfolk and Suffolk, and on the Welsh border. Almost without exception they are noble pieces of work, often painted or coloured, and whilst the wholesale destruction of the roods was ordered under Edward VI, the screens themselves were never forbidden. Many counties had their own local style but all were quite remarkable for their craftsmanship. Those of the West Country possibly excel and there are still about a hundred and fifty perfect examples in Devon. Actually screen-building did not die out until Hanoverian days, but many which had survived the religious troubles were swept away in due course by the Victorian restorers.

'Doom' paintings were common in the medieval church, and these were either destroyed or covered by whitewash. In their place, early in the seventeenth century, the Ten Commandments, the Creed and the Our Father were painted in, usually at the eastern end of the chancel or on each side of the chancel arch. They still remain in many country churches. Wall-paintings from medieval days are still being discovered, some of which have sustained up to a score of coats of wash over them. It says something for the skill of the artist in mixing his colours that those remaining are almost as bright and clear as ever.

In the early churches there was virtually no seating until the fifteenth century when pews became general. The earliest types were quite plain, but eventually the ends of the pews became a feature of most churches. Many village churches have such examples of the wood-carver's art. Beautiful work, virile and bold, it sometimes displays a gorgeous sense of humour.

Fortunately some medieval glass survived the reformers. Some was hidden, some escaped because it had heraldic designs rather than religious motifs or illustrations.

The reign of James I brought a revolt against the coarse carving which had prevailed for so long. Inigo Jones, master mason at Whitehall, became known for his work, particularly the great sepulchral monuments and undoubtedly he considerably influenced those geniuses Wren and Gibbons who were to follow hard upon his heels. Other master masons became famous for their superb work, so often shown on tombs and monuments. Nicholas Stone, and later his son, were typical of those who imbibed foreign techniques and improved upon them.

The arts took on a more classical aspect. The sarcophagus type of tomb made its appearance with busts and allegorical figures, a style which excluded the more extravagant signs of devout symbolism, due possibly to a fear of association or sympathy with popery. The cross as an emblem was not so common and the urn (oddly enough a relic of paganism) took its place. The whole period from 1603 to 1688 became an age of allegory, violently interrupted by the Civil War, the causes of which were both political and religious. The fury of the fanatical section of the Puritans and their urge for austerity created further havoc and destruction in the churches. By reason of the political atmosphere the results were even more devasting than was apparent in the Reformation. Churches were cleared of everything which offended, and a great many items that could be removed were destroyed. All that remained was defaced or painted over. The effect of Puritanism became evident. The church became a preaching house.

The hour-glass or sand-glass was certainly known before the Reformation, but was used rather by individuals for private devotions than for public services. In the seventeenth century they came into regular use as a sermon timer, some of them running for an hour and a half.

Austere tombs became the vogue. That of Speaker Lenthall in Burford Church, Oxfordshire, which bears the words *Vermis sum*— 'I am a worm', was perhaps an extreme case, but still typical.

The Restoration of 1660 at last brought some measure of religious toleration and soon afterwards the churches began to change. Instead of the bare preaching place and the comparative sparsity of furniture, by Georgian times churches had a superfluity of woodwork and monuments.

In an effort to make the interiors more comfortable and less austere, enclosed pews which excluded draughts and gave a modicum of privacy became general. Those which were high-backed became known as 'horse-box' pews. Many pews of the squires or lords of the manor were quite elaborate. Often very large, they were fitted with cushions, carpets and sometimes even a stove. Many were ill-conceived and ugly, others had some artistic merit.

Preaching had become general in the fifteenth century, but many churches had managed without a pulpit. In 1603, however, churchwardens were ordered to provide one in every church. The high pews, and also the fact that to accommodate the larger congregations galleries had been added, made a higher pulpit a necessity. So the two and three-deckers made their appearance. There were three positions, one above the other. The clerk occupied the lowest part, the reader the next and the third and highest portion was occupied by the preacher. Few of these have much to commend them, but the many single-style Jacobean pulpits, complete with an ornately carved sounding-board above, are superb.

Hatchments—usually lozenge-shaped boards—which bore the coat of arms of a distinguished person, were a common form of adornment in churches before the Commonwealth, but were not encouraged in that period. However, they reappeared in the Stuart and Georgian churches.

The royal arms had become common in churches during the reign of Henry VIII, possibly as a symbol of the royal supremacy: Edward VI had had them installed in place of the rood. After the Restoration, however, the placing of the arms became compulsory and a wide range of styles including some very fine examples remain, some are painted above the chancel arch, others on board. Some are of plaster, coloured and gilded. More rare are those integrated with the ironwork of chancel gates. All these things helped to bring back colour and dignity to the Georgian church.

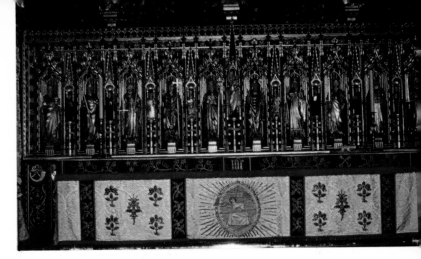

The interior of the medieval church was a blaze of colour. At the back of the chancel the reredos, often made of precious metal, set off the altar with its cloths, hangings and plate; the walls were painted, as was the arch above with its doom picture, whilst the crowning glory was the beautifully carved and coloured screen

With the Restoration, there was a steady development of the Classical architectural style. Christopher Wren, Grinling Gibbons, Nicholas Hawksmoor and many more masters of their craft quickly made their mark. The exquisite wood-carving of Grinling Gibbons set a very high standard, and other craftsmen worked towards such perfection.

After the Great Fire, Wren alone was responsible for more than fifty churches in the City of London, in addition to St Paul's Cathedral. There was a spate of building which called for new ideas in fittings and adornments, a phase which went on until the last thirty years of the eighteenth century, when craftsmanship in all these things became supreme.

In 1818, there was considerable concern that the areas of the country in which there had been an increase in population had insufficient churches. The Church Building Act, therefore, came into being and 214 churches were built, of which thirty were in and around London. These were known as Waterloo churches because they were erected soon after the great victory. Some of the churches built within the terms of the million-pound grant made by Parliament in 1818 were quite outstanding both in design and conception.

Even though they were built to a price, and in districts which, owing to the Industrial Revolution, had considerably increased their population, their architecture became very much an affair of personalities, as people like Gibbs, Archer and Hawksmoor took up the challenge.

The Victorian Age was a golden period of English church building, comparable with the fifteenth century. The designs of the new churches were often original and good, as is evident in some of these in London and the provinces. Architects included: Pugin (mostly Roman Catholic); Pearson; Butterfield; Gilbert Scott; Thomas White, who was responsible for many Georgian churches in Worcester; and James Gibbs for many in Derbyshire and Staffordshire (he was also responsible for the steeple at St Martin-in-the-Fields, London), to name a few.

This new surge received its impetus from the Evangelical Movement, which was led by the Wesleys, Wilberforce, the Frys and Whitefields. Then followed the Tractarian or Oxford Movement which received its momentum from John Keble. The term 'Tractarianism' came into use about 1833, and referred to a religious breakaway in which divines like Pusey, Newman and other Oxford churchmen played a prominent part. Among other things they advocated a higher degree of ceremonial in worship and their enthusiasm put new activity into the Church, although the secession to Rome of some of their more prominent members showed its Roman Catholic tendencies.

Victorian prosperity was reflected in the furnishings and fittings of the churches. Where there were wealthy patrons, ostentatious marble pulpits and other items made their appearance. Many of the tombs and monuments tended to become bizarre and over-ostentatious. Certainly the Victorians restored many lovely ancient churches almost out of existence, but they also conserved much which had been allowed to fall into ruin. Their admiration for fourteenth-century Decorated and Early Perpendicular styles resulted in mass production of Suburban Gothic.

Churches were built with adequate seating to accommodate the vastly increased population. In this era, the priest once again took his place in the chancel and other parts of the church came into constant use.

In the fifteenth century, so the cynic says, people used their church for worship. In the twentieth century, more people than ever are interested in the ancient buildings but few remain to pray. Nevertheless, in England there is a wealth of ancient churches. The splendid architecture, the superb carving and woodwork, the styles and variety of tombs and monuments, almost always the work of local craftsmen, are a unique heritage.

1 *Reredos, Ripon Cathedral*

2 *Christ of the Trades was a popular subject for wall-painting. This little picture in the church of Breage, Cornwall, was brought to light in 1891, having been covered, it is believed, for three hundred years*

3 *The cross over the chancel, Chittlehampton*

4 *The screen at Burrington, Devon. The pomegranates in the design help to date it, for they were borne in the arms of the Kings of Granada which first appear in England when Catherine of Aragon married Henry VIII in 1509*

In the sixth and seventh centuries saints played an important part in the lives of the people. There were saints for every calling, every ailment, almost every circumstance. St Christopher, patron saint of travellers, was very popular and his likeness was often on the north wall opposite the main door of the church. The most popular dedication was to the Blessed Virgin. In Devon it became a tradition to paint saints on the lower part of the screen, with males to the north of the chancel door and females to the south

5 (opposite) *Reredos, Shipton Sollars, Gloucester*

6 (opposite) *Base of the screen, Ipplepen, Devon*

8

In the twelfth century the great monastic Orders increased both their numbers and their influence. Following the building of Waverley in 1128 the Cistercians alone built five hundred other monastic churches during the century. Fountains Abbey gives an idea of their scale and craftsmanship; the nave was 358 ft long, the cellarium a mere 300 ft

7, 8 *The ruins of Fountains Abbey, and the cellarium*

7

10

Screens were used to divide the chancel
from the nave, much as in the Orthodox
Church. Except in large churches the work
was usually done by local village craftsmen. Most screens were originally
surmounted by a loft and rood until their
wholesale destruction by order in the
reign of Edward VI

11

9 (opposite) *Vaulting of the screen at
Chulmleigh, Devon*

10 *The screen at Chulmleigh*

11 *Rood-loft, Atherington, Devon*

12 *Screen at Cullompton, Devon*

12

13 *This superb and unusual chancel screen at Staunton
Harold, Leicestershire, made in the eighteenth century, is
believed to be the work of Robert Bakewell*

14 *Choir-screen at Ripon Cathedral*

14

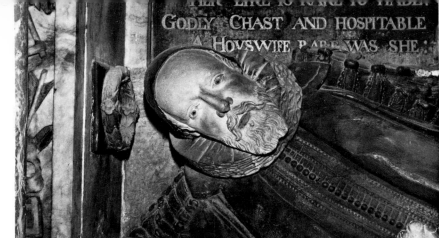

15

17

18

15, 16 The detail in the earlier memorials is shown in the Bluett tomb in Holcombe Rogus, Devon

17 The wealthy often had their tombs prepared in their lifetime, such as this tomb at Miserden, Gloucestershire, attributed to the master craftsman, Nicholas Stone

18 A complicated wall memorial at Brent Knoll

20

20 *The Dodderidge tomb in Exeter Cathedral, where the skull was used to emphasize the finality of death*

21 *For sheer simplicity this tomb at Chipping Norton, Oxford, is hard to surpass*

22 *The Fettiplace Memorial, Swinbrook, Oxford*

23 *The flamboyant memorial of Earl Fauconberg handing his coronet to his son. Coxwold, Yorkshire*

20

22

21

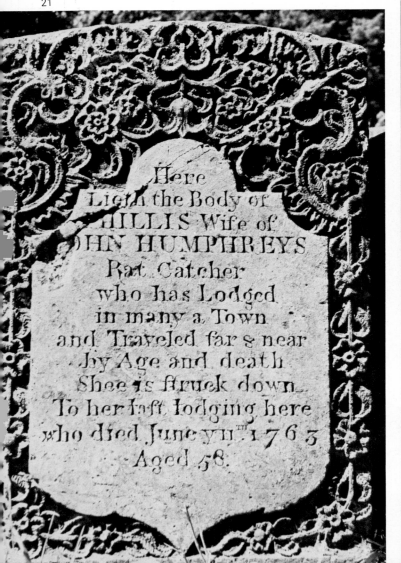

Here
Lieth the Body of
HILLIS Wife of
OHN HUMPHREYS
Rat Catcher
who has Lodged
in many a Town
and Traveled far & near
by Age and death
Shee is struck down
To her last lodging here
who died June y ii 1763
Aged 58

24

In Georgian times there was an extravagant use of woodwork and carving. Some of the horse-box pews which were popular were extravagantly carved and even fitted with a stove. These box pews made higher pulpits a necessity, so two and three-deckers were constructed

24 *Private pew at Kirkby Malham, Yorkshire*

25 *Lord of the Manor's pew, Wensley, Yorkshire*

26 *Squire's pew, Selworthy, Somerset*

27 *Three-decker pulpit in the diminutive church of Mungrisdale, Cumberland*

28

Early seats in churches were of the plain, backless, bench type. By the fifteenth century seating had become general and the pew ends offered splendid chances for the fine wood-carving of the period. Hour-glasses made their appearance largely because of the long sermons

28 *Pew end at Wiggenhall, Norfolk*

29 *High Bickington, Devon*

30 *Elaborately carved pulpit and sounding-board, Croscombe, Somerset*

31 *Metal arm to carry the hour-glass, Tawstock, Devon*

32 (opposite) *Pulpit at Ipplepen*

29

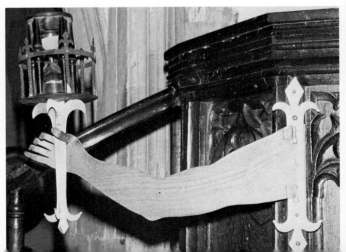

There remaineth
therefore a rest to the
people of God.
Heb.IV.9.

37

Although the royal coat of arms had been displayed previously in churches, it only became general after Henry VIII declared himself Head of the Church. It became compulsory after the Restoration. Hatchments became popular in Georgian times

39

36 (opposite) 'Sentences of Scripture decently flourished', Hawkshead

37 The arms of Charles I at Boconnoc, Cornwall, are quite large, due probably to the fact that the King held his court there during the campaign in the West, 1643

38 Georgian arms in plaster, Newlyn East, Cornwall

39 Hatchment at Greystoke, Cumberland

DIEV · ET · MON · DROIT

38

40

41

40 *One of the panels on the pulpit at East Budleigh, Devon, depicting the stoning of St Stephen, carved early in the nineteenth century*

41 *Modern decoration of the choir pews, High Bickington, Devon*

MARTIN BLINDHEIM M.A.

NORTH OF THE BALTIC

For a long time Scandinavia was the last and most feared pagan corner of western Europe. During the Migrations hordes of warriors spread all over Europe. In the Viking Age new hordes ravaged the coasts of the North Sea and the Baltic and ultimately settled in the new territories. By way of the Russian rivers they tried to conquer Constantinople and they also reached the Mediterranean from the Atlantic. They founded kingdoms in the British Isles, colonized Iceland and Greenland and tried to settle in North America around AD 1000.

The Scandinavians were closely related to each other. They spoke practically the same language. They believed in the same gods and had more or less the same way of living. Geographically, Viking-Age Scandinavia fell into three parts, roughly corresponding with what we today call Norway, Sweden and Denmark. Finland is not Scandinavian; the people there are ethnically different and they speak another language.

Christian Europe must have regarded the Vikings as wild hordes. But it should not be forgotten that the Viking society was well organized and had its own as yet unwritten laws.

The increasing contact with Christian Europe had its growing effect on Scandinavia. Already in the second half of the tenth century Denmark was converted to Christianity, and the ideas began to penetrate into the coastal districts of Norway. In the year 1000 Iceland was christened by an act of their parliament (the Alting). Sweden followed later, in the eleventh century. The most impressive monument of the conversion of Denmark is King Harald Bluetooth's memorial stone, the oldest Christian monument in Scandinavia, raised about AD 980 at Jellinge Church in Jutland. On one side there is a representation of the most important of all Christian symbols—the crucifixion. Along the western coast of Norway slender high crosses of stone were raised at joint points of communication. The oldest Christian church so far found has been excavated at the outpost of the Nordic area, Greenland. Tjodhilde, the wife of the chieftain Eric the Red, built this tiny church of turf and wood at the dawn of the eleventh century.

In Norway people gave way to the new faith by King Olav Haraldson's martyr's death on the battlefield of Stiklestad in 1030. He rapidly came to be venerated throughout the Nordic

world. It seems that this was partly due to the fact that St Olav stood for many of the same features as the old pagan gods. Somewhat later Sweden and Denmark found their national royal saints in St Erik and St Knud respectively.

The first churches in Scandinavia were made of wood. These so-called stave churches had their vertically placed walls embedded in the ground, according to old building customs all over the North Sea area. The successors of these churches were the real Norwegian stave churches from the twelfth to the thirteenth centuries in which the whole construction is placed on a stone foundation. Altogether twenty-five of these spectacular buildings have been preserved. They are without doubt the most important Scandinavian contribution to European architecture. In a way one might say that a stave church could be regarded as a huge piece of sculpture. The ornamentation of the oldest eleventh-century stave church doorways must be regarded as the latest descendants of the Viking animal styles. The twelfth-century doorways on the other hand show a happy combination of native traditions and Romanesque impulses from Lombard and English art in the second quarter of the century. A special group of doorways are narrative and depict the Germanic hero Sigurd's fight with the dragon Favne and the hero Gunnar's death in the snake-pit.

The art of hewing stone for building purposes was introduced in the eleventh century, and during the twelfth and thirteenth centuries churches of stone and brick were built all over Scandinavia according to general north European principles. Most of them were small parish churches. They had narrow doorways and few and narrow windows to keep the buildings as warm as possible in the cold winter climate. Only in Norway were the majority of the new churches still stave churches.

The twelfth century witnessed the construction of cathedrals as well as the founding of archbishoprics in Lund, Trondheim and Uppsala. Little by little Scandinavia became not only an active part of the European Church; their civilization was also Europeanized. The most important ecclesiastical Orders got their houses in the Scandinavian countries. Only one Order was founded in the North—the Order of S. Birgitta. From Vadstena in Sweden her fame spread far and wide over Europe.

The altars were certainly not always as pompous in their furnishings as in western Europe. But it is a fact that more has been preserved from the Middle Ages in the North than elsewhere. The stylistic features testify to impulses from the South to the Baltic North and to a strong Western influence to Norway across the North Sea. Hundreds of twelfth and thirteenth-century wooden altar sculptures and crucifixions can still be seen in the churches or in the museums of Scandinavia. Later sculptures may be counted by the thousands.

2 *Excavation plan of the Church of Tjorhilde, wife of Eric the Red, in Greenland. The tiny size of the church is clearly shown by the skeletons in the surrounding graveyard*

3 *Memorial stone to Harold Bluetooth at Jellinge*

4 *All that remains of a high stone cross from Toten, Oppland, apparently depicting scenes from the Nativity*

3

4

Of special interest among the *vasa sacra* (holy vessels) is a group of reliquaries in gilt hammered-copper in the shape of houses. Dragon heads on the gables testify to traditions from the heads on the stave churches and the Viking ships. More or less the same technique was employed on the splendid so-called 'golden altars'—gilt altar frontals found in Denmark. They went out of date in the Early Gothic period. At the same time painted altar frontals came into use in Norway and became immensely popular. These English-influenced paintings from the thirteenth and fourteenth centuries should be regarded as a parallel to the painted altar frontals of Spain and northern Italy.

Through baptism people became members of the Christian Church. Consequently the font was a very important piece of church furniture. It was placed near the western door. In the beginning it was a wooden basin; later it was carved out of stone with a cover of wood or metal. A very peculiar group are the numerous twelfth-century granite fonts from Jutland. Another and even more spectacular group are the chalk fonts of Gotland with their sumptuous pictorial carvings.

A few Romanesque chairs and benches were without doubt meant for the bishop at the inauguration of the new church.

The fifteenth and sixteenth centuries saw a strong economic and political rise for the Baltic North and a corresponding decline for the Atlantic North, including the Western and Atlantic Isles. The north German influence was overwhelming and Church art was completely dominated by it.

In the 1520s and 1530s the Reformation reached Scandinavia. In most places the old priests continued in their offices but the liturgy was changed according to the Lutheran rite. Little by little altar sculptures disappeared from most places, but the crucifixes were not touched. Only the main altar remained with the most important of the holy vessels.

A short period of iconoclasm followed the Reformation, but soon architects, carvers and painters introduced the Renaissance and Baroque styles to the North. Singing and reading became important elements of the service. Consequently the number of windows grew and they were made much bigger. As the Lutheran service was very long it became important to make the churches both lighter and warmer in the dark, cold Nordic winter. The European architects working in the richer parts of Scandinavia had to take notice of this problem, which really could not be solved before the twentieth century. From the richer areas the new ideas spread to the most remote parts of the Nordic world.

Soon pictorial art again penetrated the churches. Almost obligatory was a huge altar-piece with scenes from the Passion. In the nave one would find the pulpit. Benches covered the floor

5 *Cross over a grave in the churchyard at Bru, carved about the year 1000*

6 *Detail of carving on the door of the stave church at Urnes*

7 *Bricked-up south door at Velbyk showing the influence of the Romanesque style in the carved stone*

8 *This Crucifixion from the Fana Church has a striking similarity to the Plague Cross of Cologne*

9 *Painted altar frontal from Tresford Church*

and galleries ran along the walls. The woodwork was richly carved and painted. There were pictures of the Apostles, Evangelists, Prophets and allegorical scenes at the appropriate symbolic places. On the whole one is justified in saying that all the more important spiritual and artistic movements which in the post-Reformation centuries marked the Germanic South had their counterparts in the North. Scandinavia had to wait till the twentieth century—to be quite correct, until the decades after the Second World War—to give birth to architectural and ornamental conceptions of general interest. However, it should be remembered that what is now called Scandinavian Design or Scandinavian Modern is firmly based on ideas and works of German, French and American origin.

Designers and architects all over Scandinavia took part in this movement and are still doing so. Perhaps a place of prominence, at least in the beginning, should be granted to Finnish architects and Danish designers. It could be said that

the basic ideas are simplification and lines naturally adaptable to all the revolutionary new materials and techniques. It also seems obvious that among the many sources of inspiration are old building traditions, old handicrafts and forms found in Nature itself.

The shapes of modern churches are manifold. In some instances stave churches and old boat-houses have inspired steep, pointed silhouettes and a lofty triangular interior. Else-where the shapes are completely unorthodox without any special architectural division between nave and chancel, so that the service of God shall take place in the middle of the congregation as in the first Christian times. A typical feature every-where is that the interior is bright and fully lighted. There are no dark corners and no place for romantic mysticism.

Present-day architects and designers in Scandinavia are again specializing as in the Middle Ages, but with a different background and with new ideas.

5

6

10 *Elaborately carved altar from Lisbjerg. Although Northern European style has obviously influenced the carver in his composition, the design of the border is still traditionally Scandinavian*

11 *Detail of effigy on the tombstone of Queen Margaret*

12 *Folding altar-piece from St Knud's Church in Odense*

13 *Stave church at Borgund*

14, 15 *Interior of the wooden churches at Hopperstad and Urnes*

14   15

16 *Virgin with Child. Hove Church, Soga*

17 *St Olaf—patron saint of Norway*

18 *This altar triptych of St Canute shows a marked contrast of styles between the carved central figure and the paintings on the side panels*

19 *The simplicity of nineteenth-century Finnish church building can be seen in this picture of the church at Lemi*

20 *Carved and painted interior of the church at Kvikne, Norway*

21 *The Church of Hollola, Finland, showing the east end. The tower to the south is of completely different style, recalling some of the churches of the Eastern Orthodox rite whose missionaries journeyed to Lapland in the fourteenth century*

19

21

20

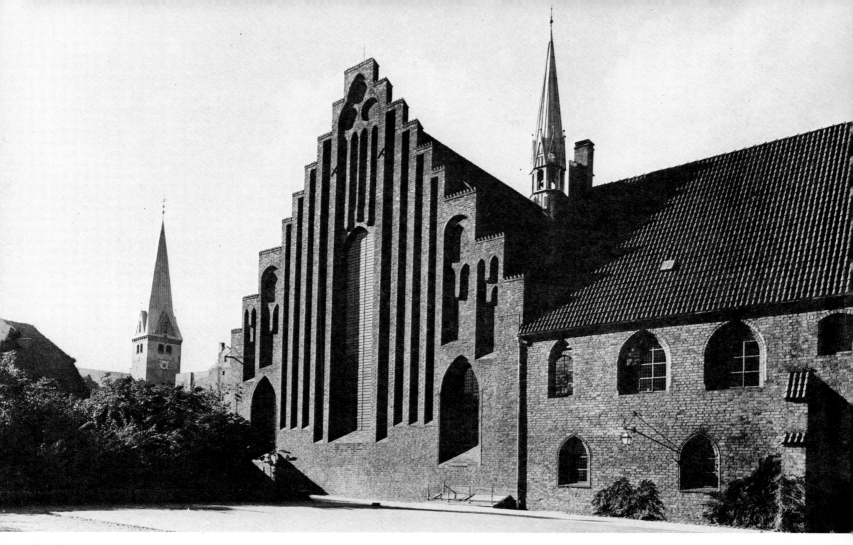

22 *Interior of the Church of Vantor, Stockholm*

23 *St Mary's, Helsingfors*

24 *Interior of the Church of Allerslev; the Baroque influence can clearly be seen*

25 *Detail of the altar at Vantor*

26 *Interior of the St Halvards Catholic Church. The absence of hangings and the contrast of materials—brick, mosaic and wood—are fundamental to modern Scandinavian design*

27 *Concentrated floodlighting is a feature of the Kaleva Church, Tampere, in Finland though whether it achieves a spiritual result is perhaps doubtful*

DR PETER CANNON-BROOKES M.A.

BAROQUE AND ROCOCO

December 1563 saw the last session of the Council of Trent and the definition of a new role for the arts, as servants of the Counter-Reformation. With the exception of Venice, Rome had dominated Italian religious art since the beginning of the second decade of the century and, although the Sack of Rome in 1527 temporarily interrupted this pattern, the papal court maintained this position until the end of the third quarter of the seventeenth century. During this time the Baroque style was evolved and reached its climax in Italy, and Rome remained throughout the focal point. Compared with the brilliant hedonism of the courts of Julius II and Leo X, those of Paul IV (1555–9) and Pius IV (1559–65) represent the opposite extreme, and reforming zeal with an almost grim austerity and asceticism was the order of the day.

A religious work of art, according to the reformers, should be easily intelligible, realistic and an emotional stimulus to piety, and these demands were all totally opposed to the courtly mannerist style with its emphasis on elegance and sophistication. The reformers who drew up the decrees were heavily influenced by medieval ideas, and it is probable that, in their opposition to Mannerism, they had in mind the realism of Late Gothic art. However this desire for clarity and intelligibility was by no means confined to the reformers, as a number of artists towards the end of the second quarter had come to recognize the basic unsuitability of the mannerist style for religious art, and as early as the 1550s a conscious re-assessment of the High Renaissance was under way in Florence.

Integral with the evolution of the Counter-Reformation was the emergence of the new Orders, and St Philip Neri's Oratory and St Ignatius of Loyola's Society of Jesus played an increasingly important role. The Oratory was formally recognized in 1575 and the Church of S. Maria in Vallicella was assigned to it, while after many vicissitudes St Ignatius's constitutions were finally confirmed in 1591. The new Orders set great store by preaching and the large congregations they attracted led to the erection of a series of enormous churches specially designed for this purpose. Vignola began the mother-church of the Jesuits, the Gesù, in 1568, and, as befitted the strict quasi-military discipline of the Order, the vaults of the church were whitewashed. The present decorations were begun almost a century later and would have horrified St Ignatius.

Official papal taste up until the death of Paul V in 1621 was conservative and often thoroughly prosaic, and successive pontiffs remained far more interested in the subject-matter of their commissions than in artistic merit. The series of martyrdoms painted by Pomerancio in S. Stefano Rotonda are conspicuous for their nauseating realism, while the majority of the sculpture on the tombs in the Pauline and Sistine Chapels in S. Maria Maggiore sink to the level of pure propaganda. However, it is in this realism that the roots of the Baroque lie, and the Early Baroque sculptors such as Camillo Mariani and Pietro Bernini took the first steps. The first precise indications of a new spirit are to be found in the 1590s, with the paintings of the Carracci in Bologna and the buildings of Ricchino and Maderno. The façade of the Gesù, designed by Giacomo della Porta, provides a revealing contrast to Carlo Maderno's façade of S. Susanna of 1595–1603, and, while the effect of the former is essentially one of austerity and flatness, in the latter there is a progressive movement and concentration of decoration towards the centre of the building. The whole structure of Maderno's façade is conceived in strongly sculptural terms and there is a new vigour and forcefulness in the composition.

The new spirit revealed by the art of c. 1600 was the culmination of a long process. After the hammer-blows of the Reformation the Roman Catholic Church remained on the defensive until the Council of Trent, but during the third quarter of the century, spearheaded by the Jesuits, it returned to the offensive. By the 1590s large areas previously Protestant had been regained, and there was a general feeling that the most rigorous phase of the Counter-Reformation was over. The popes, tending to be elderly and conservative, felt this last, and even Paul V (d. 1621) is seen as a transitional figure. But Gianlorenzo Bernini's bust of his nephew Cardinal Scipione Borghese reveals a plump, jovial, pleasure-loving patron of the arts such as would have been unthinkable before 1600. Gianlorenzo Bernini is the key figure of the High Baroque, and it is his genius, above all, which gives the period its distinctive flavour. An architect and painter as well as sculptor and brilliant decorator, he has left a bigger impression on Rome than any other single man. None of this would have been possible without patrons of exceptional vision and determination, and Bernini found these in Urban VIII (1623–44) and Alexander VII (1655–67).

The essential qualities of the High Baroque, with its dynamism and forceful handling of compositional elements, reflects the self-assurance of the Roman Catholic Church in Italy at a time when central Europe was in the turmoil of the Thirty Years War. It has been said that the Baroque period is not conspicuous for its spirituality, but under that self-assurance lies a very deep piety and Bernini developed the ideas of the Counter-Reformation as far as they could be accepted in Italy. The search for emotional stimuli to piety reached unparalleled heights in his hands and S. Theresa in the Cornaro Chapel floats in space, as if frozen into marble at the climax of an orgiastic frenzy. The extreme realism and sensuality of this group is deliberate and intended to inspire the worshipper to share the ecstasy of the saint.

These ideas are developed on a larger scale in his church designs, and in S. Andrea al Quirinale the execution of St Andrew takes place in the painted altar-piece while a stucco figure of the saint floats on clouds in a niche cut into the pediment over the entrance to the sanctuary. The dome of the congregation space symbolizes heaven and thus the saint, after his martyrdom, is seen passing up into heaven. This means that the entire space of the church is included within the action and the worshipper is psychologically involved in the mystery. However, the extreme illusionism and theatrical lighting of the Cornaro Chapel and the Cathedra Petri found no followers in Italy and Bernini's real artistic heirs were the Asam brothers in Germany.

Despite the daring of Bernini's illusionism he remained firmly wedded to the Classical tradition of architecture and its system of modules. Francesco Borromini on the other hand adopted a non-anthropomorphic system based on angular relationships, akin to that employed by Gothic architects, and his church of S. Ivo della Sapienza has a ground-plan based on a six-pointed star. The later façade of S. Carlo alle Quattro Fontane is one of his masterpieces, and the interplay of curves and sharp angles give it an intense liveliness which, though different from Bernini, is again wholly Baroque in its effect.

During the last quarter of the seventeenth century Rome lost her dominant role except for sculpture, where the sensuality of Bernini was rejected in favour of the much more restrained Baroque Classicism stemming from Algardi. Paradoxically this was the period of the great cycles of vault decorations in the Roman churches, which had been initiated by Pietro da Cortona with his decoration of S. Maria in Vallicella, and the plain whitewashed vaults of the reformers' churches were replaced by huge illusionistic frescoes framed by gilt stuccoes. Gaulli's 'Adoration of the Name of Jesus' on the vault of the Gesù, where the figures spill out from the frame into the body of the church, owes its inspiration to Bernini, but Andrea Pozzo's 'Allegory of the Missionary Work of the Jesuits' on the vault of S. Ignazio relies for its effect on the overwhelming illusionistic rendering of the painted architecture. Padre Pozzo settled in Vienna in 1704 and his frescoes there did much to encourage the Austrian taste for such grandiloquent decorations.

1 *The façade of the Gesù, Rome*

In Italy the lead in architecture passed to the minor centres, in particular Turin. Guarino Guarini further developed the non-anthropomorphic system of Borromini and replaced his solid vaults with open diaphanous systems of ribs such as the dome of SS. Sindone in Turin. Unfortunately all Guarini's longitudinally planned churches have been destroyed, but their designs, engraved in his *Architettura Civile*, provided the starting-point for the activity of the Dientzenhofer family in Bohemia and Franconia, and eventually for Balthasar Neumann, the greatest of all German eighteenth-century architects. The influence of French Classicism became increasingly strong in Italy from the late seventeenth century as the political power of France increased, and this is reflected in the work of one of the most brilliant and eclectic of all Italian architects—Filippo Juvara. The cool classicism of the Superga outside Turin is typical of the period, but the changed status of Italy is forcibly revealed by the fact that it is clearly inspired by the great northern abbeys such as Melk. Shortly after 1700 the centre of gravity of the Baroque was to be found north of the Alps.

The seventeenth century in Italy was a period when artistic expression was on a large scale, spiritually if not always physically; a heroic period with an emphasis laid on the qualities of grandeur and monumentality. Man's vision of God tended to be cast in this mould and it is not surprising that small intimate objects were of relatively little importance compared with the large-scale religious complexes of the times. The sense of victory over Protestantism in the late sixteenth century was replaced at the end of the seventeenth century by a new sense of victory—that over the infidel. The Turks had been repelled from the gates of Vienna and the Austrian armies had begun to capture huge areas of eastern Europe, while Jesuit missionaries were meeting with unparalleled (though in fact short-lived) successes in the Far East. This optimism is strangely at variance with the increasing political impotence of the papacy, and it is revealing that as early as 1648 the Thirty Years War could be ended by the Peace of Westphalia without papal participation in the negotiations.

Recovery from the devastation of the Thirty Years War took a long time in central Europe, and artistic activity was minimal until the 1680s. The sheer scale of the reconstruction involved is often little appreciated, but in areas such as Bohemia the vast majority of the churches had to be heavily restored or entirely rebuilt. At first the scene in southern Germany and Austria was dominated by Italian and Italo-Swiss architects and craftsmen, such as Carlo Domenico Lucchese from Tessin who was responsible for the superb stuccoes at Speinshart, while the mainly Protestant areas of northern Germany continued to look to the Netherlands for inspiration. During the last decade of the seventeenth century the first important Baroque architects born north of the Alps began their activity; this occurred about a decade earlier in Austria, and in particular Salzburg, than elsewhere in the Germanic lands.

Fischer von Erlach was trained in Italy at the time when the great cycles of vault decorations were being executed in the Roman churches. Soon he came to appreciate the advantages to be gained from closer co-ordination, with the architecture, sculpture and frescoes all planned together instead of decoration being added to an already completed structure. Such ideas were not entirely new, as Bernini and even Raphael had done just this on previous occasions, but the *Gesamtkunstwerk* became an increasingly important concept. In the Karlskirche Fischer von Erlach attempted to lay the foundations of an imperial Northern Baroque style of architecture, but his plans were altered by his son after his death to conform to the change in taste which occurred in the second quarter. Monumentality and grandeur were no longer required; instead the emphasis was on lightness and surface decoration, as represented by the architecture of Hildebrandt. However, this was as close as the majority of Austrian architecture, outside the Tyrol, ever approached the Rococo which flowered in southern Germany.

Cosmas Damian Asam and his brother Egid Quirin were sent in 1711 to Rome for their training, and they seized upon Bernini's theatrical handling of space and light. After their return to Bavaria they began a series of brilliant decorative ensembles, of which the abbey church at Weltenburg (begun 1718) is justly one of the most famous. The architecture, sculpture and painting are combined to produce an overwhelming theatrical effect. The life-size equestrian figure of St George on the high altar transfixes the dragon with his lance, and the princess recoils in terror. Behind him the fresco of the Assumption of the Virgin is strongly lit from concealed windows so that the central *tableau vivant* is silhouetted against the bright colours behind, while additional realism is provided by details such as the goose at the feet of St Martin which hisses at the dragon. Throughout there is a synthesis of the native German Gothic tradition of realism with the overwhelming theatrical effects of Bernini, so as to make the religious experience as intensely real as possible. The dynamism of the composition and the strength of the illusion are essentially Baroque in spirit but, as in Austria, a change in spirit is felt in the second quarter, though the Asams continued working in the Baroque style for the rest of their careers.

The Rococo takes two forms in Germany, and the basically French-inspired style, as exemplified by Cuvilles, was favoured by the Bavarian court and the great ecclesiastical princes of Franconia and the Middle Rhine. The native Bavarian style,

3 *The interior of S. Andrea al Quirinale, Rome, looking towards the sanctuary with the figure of St Andrew clearly visible*

4 *Bust of Cardinal Scipio Borghese by Bernini, first version, in the Borghese Gallery, Rome*

however, as evolved by the Zimmermann brothers, was most popular in the country areas, particularly in southern Bavaria and Swabia where abbots tended to be local men and rarely the scions of great families. The taste for naturalistic details, as seen in the work of the Asams, is much more pronounced in that of the Zimmermanns. At Steinhausen (begun 1728) stucco doves perch in the windows while bees and insects wander through the foliage of the capitals. The emphasis is on lightness and a certain lyrical charm, and the sense of dynamic structure characteristic of the Baroque is replaced by an insubstantial ensemble in which the architectural elements lose their structural significance and become more decorative than functional in appearance. This change in values is reflected in the abstract forms taken by the windows and, at Die Wies, the extraordinary series of penetrations through the vault of the sanctuary which entirely negate any sense of structural solidarity.

Die Wies was entirely built from the offerings of simple pilgrims, and although it became very famous it always remained a people's pilgrimage shrine. Just as with Late Gothic sculpture, the realism and naturalistic details of the ensemble enabled unsophisticated people to identify themselves with the mysteries of the Church. This sense of personal identification is taken to its conclusion at Birnau on Lake Constance where Götz included in one of his frescoes a mirror so that the pilgrim, standing on the correct spot on the floor of the church, would see himself in heaven receiving the benediction of the Virgin! Such an idea in the twentieth century would be rejected as a vulgar gimmick, but in the eighteenth century it fulfilled a very real desire.

Further north the pilgrimage churches, such as Vierzehn-heiligen and Gössweinstein, present a rather different picture, and there the overwhelming influence of the patron is strongly felt. Perhaps the most remarkable of the ecclesiastical patrons, after Clemens August of Cologne, were the members of the Schönborn family, headed by Lothar Franz, the Elector of Mainz, and his four nephews, all bishops. Apart from the wealth of their bishoprics, they all shared a positive passion for building and provided Neumann with his most important patrons, but the bulk of their efforts was directed not at churches but at a staggering series of palaces and castles.

It is relatively rare to find a church in which both the architecture and decoration are Rococo, the normal situation being that Rococo decoration was applied to a structure fundamentally Baroque in spirit. The dissolution of structure characteristic of Rococo architecture is, for example, much less strongly felt at Ottobeuren (by J. M. Fischer) than Steinhausen, and after about 1750 the quantity of *rocaille* decoration tends to be heavily reduced. Structural elements again become increasingly well defined until the cool clarity of churches like Neresheim is attained. This process is partly due to the influence of French Classicism, but in the 1750s J. J. Winckelmann had emerged in Dresden as the champion of that far more academic Classicism we now term Neoclassicism. The cool colours and clear-cut monumental forms in Januarius Zick's frescoes at Rot-an-der-Rot show a total rejection of the lyrical vivacity of the Rococo, and after the death of the Austrian Archduchess Maria Christina it was the Neoclassicist Canova who was commissioned to execute her tomb.

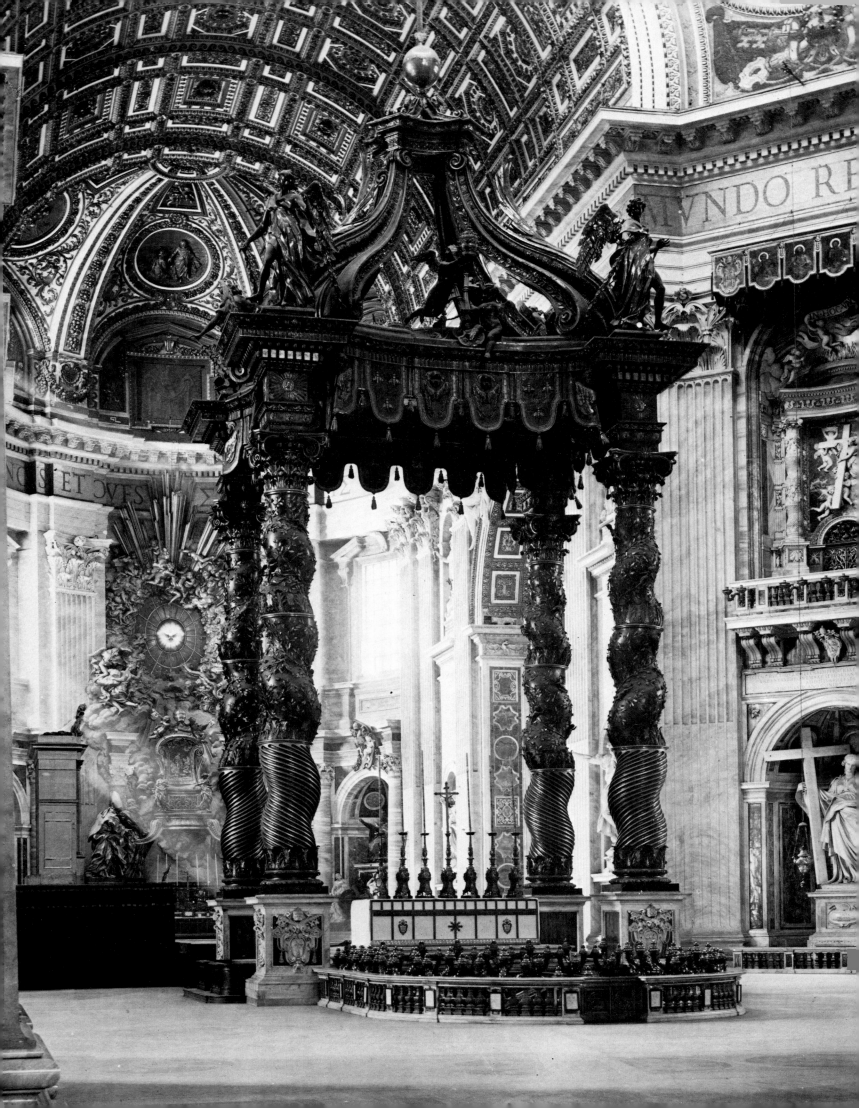

5 (preceding page) *La Confessione, St Peter's, Rome*

6 (preceding page) *Adoration of the Name of Jesus. Fresco in the ceiling of the Gesù, Rome, by Baciccia*

7 *The Ecstasy of St Theresa by Bernini, in the Cornaro Chapel, S. Maria della Vittoria, Rome. Bernini is the great transitional sculptor between the periods of Renaissance and Baroque*

8 *The façade of S. Carlo alle Quattro Fontane, Rome*

9 (opposite) *The meeting of Pope Leo I and Attila, by Algardi, St Peter's, Rome*

7

8

10

11

10, 11 *Exterior and interior views of the dome of the chapel of S. Sindone, Turin*

12 *General view of the exterior of the Superga outside Turin, showing the relationship between church and monastery*

13 *The Diamond Monstrance of 1699, now in the Treasury of Loreta, Prague. It is made of gilded silver and encrusted with over six thousand diamonds*

12

15

16 17

14 (opposite) *The exterior of Les Invalides, Paris, showing façade and dome*

15 *Conventual Church of the Most Sovereign and Military Order of the Knights of St John of Jerusalem—the Hospitallers—in Malta*

16 *General view of the Monastery of Melk, seen from the river*

17 *The façade of the Karlskirche, Vienna*

18 *High altar of the Abbey Church of Weltenberg, Bavaria, showing the central group of St George and the Dragon with the saints on either side*

19 *General view of the interior of Neresheim, Bavaria, looking towards the high altar*

20 *Stucco ceiling in the Library of the Papal Apartments, Castle of St Angelo, Rome*

19

20

21, 22 *Two frescoes of the Virgin showing the wonderful use of perspective in the dome which the Baroque painters exploited so well. The Goetz mirror for the pilgrim to see his own reflection can be clearly seen*

23 *Details of the interior of one of the windows at Steinhausen showing perched doves and the capital of a column with insects*

24 (overleaf) *High altar at Steinhausen*

25 (overleaf) *Cardinal Peter Damian; statue in the Abbey Church of Rot-am-Inn*

26 (opposite) *Fresco of Christ in the Temple, painted by Jan Zick on the vault of the Abbey Church, Rot-an-der-Rot, Bavaria*

27 *Canova's tomb of Maria Christina, Augustinerkirche, Vienna*

28 *Arms of Pope Paul III in the Palazzo della Cancelleria, Rome. It is easy to imagine how Cardinal Scipio Borghese would have appreciated such opulence*

29 (overleaf) *General view of the interior of the choir, Die Wies*

THE REV. MICHAEL BOURDEAUX M.A. B.D.

REVIVAL IN RUSSIA

'Let us throw Pushkin overboard . . .' Thus the Soviet poet, Vladimir Mayakovsky, and a group of young poets expressed the spirit of their age in a manifesto just after the 1917 Revolution. These were times of excitement, times of rebirth, times for discarding the old and setting out to fill a vast blank canvas with a many-hued, intricate, new design. In 1930 the same Mayakovsky shot himself. No event in the recent history of Russian culture more poignantly underlines the failure of the Soviet Revolution to retain the spontaneous loyalty which it had generated or to further the upsurge of new creativity to which it had initially set a spark. Old literature, old art, tradition, religion were to be thrown out: but instead of the millennium came the rise of Stalinism, the purges. In a terrorized society no one was left unscathed in the 1930s: the electricity of the creative impulse was short-circuited out of public expression. A rack of loud-mouthed, uniform idolatry and self-congratulatory chauvinism enshrouded the Press. The muscular, featureless statue, hand raised in greeting to a mythical idealized future, replaced the glorious innovations of Kandinsky, Malevich and Larionov to become the palimpsest of the age.

The labour-pains of the Revolution brought forth a child fully armed into the world—but the Soviets gazed in horror and could see it only as Frankenstein's monster. 'Away with non-party writers!' said Lenin. They emigrated, wasted away in prison camps, committed suicide or were shot. An artistic spiritual vacuum was created. Its sterility was emphasized only the more when Stalin, the instrument of its creation, was himself posthumously dethroned.

The story of present-day Russian art and literature is the attempt to eradicate from the consciousness the bad dream of Stalinism and to return to the well-springs of the national culture. One is reminded of the prison experiences of Yevgenia Ginzburg which she described in her book, *Into the Whirlwind*. When her physical resources were almost exhausted, she was sent one spring into the Siberian forest to hew lumber. There she found 'that fragile miracle of nature, a sprig of cranberry, emerging from the melting ice'—succulent berries which had been blanketed at the end of the previous summer by the snow and preserved with enhanced flavour until revealed by the thaw. Their vitamins saved her life, but she saw in them a

1 Y. V. VUCHETICH: Beat Swords into Ploughshares, *bronze, 1957*

2 PAVEL KORIN (*born 1892*): Metropolitan Trifon. *Figure later incorporated into the unfinished painting,* Requiem. *Korin exhibited in New York, May 1965—a rare example of the Soviet Government giving permission for religious work to be shown*

symbolism beyond their function as a panacea of nature: 'The intoxicating aroma was that of victory over suffering and winter.'

Beneath the enveloping snow of a cruel winter, the rich tradition of Russian letters, art, religion and history has been preserved. When the history of Russian twentieth-century culture comes finally to be written, the keynote will be continuity rather than change. In poetry, Boris Pasternak, Marina Tsvetaeva and Anna Akhmatova, all educated before the Revolution, continued to express and enrich the traditional values, despite the severest official pressures against them. In painting, Pavel Korin did the same. They were all Christians. That they should now have become the inspiration of the younger generation, of the imprisoned writer, Sinyavsky, and the literary underground, is entirely symptomatic of the temper of the age.

The new Soviet festivals which the State has tried to impose on the people from above have not become ingrained in the hearts of the millions who remain loyal to the revered and variegated traditions of old. The only lasting effect of the attempt to destroy the past has been to weld the sensitive thinker more closely to it. Nowhere has this been more dramatically manifested than in the battle to preserve Russia's architectural heritage. Since the Revolution thousands of churches, repositories of the finest inspiration of the old Russian architect, painter, mosaic artist and wood-carver, have perished. Some fell to the German invader, others suffered irreparably through being converted into warehouses and tractor sheds; many more were destroyed in the name of enlightened urban reconstruction for the socialist future. This process was not halted until 1964: even now there is no guarantee that similar instances will not recur. Yet fresh hope has been provided by the foundation in 1965 of the Society for the Protection of Historical Monuments, which is now a focal point around which popular support can be rallied against the inroads of atheist bureaucracy. It is unique in being supported both by the masses and the intelligentsia. One of the most attractive summer pursuits for the Soviet university student, deprived of the possibility of foreign travel, is to organize expeditions deep into the remote regions of the Soviet Union to seek out forgotten ancient churches. When found, they are charted, drawn and described with loving care. Spectacular successes are reported both in the popular Press and erudite journals and the pledge is publicly taken never to allow Russia's priceless heritage to be thus threatened again.

Nowhere is the longing to establish continuity with the past more notable than in the world of art. There are many who want to experiment again with what was being done in the

3 B. ZHUTKOVSKY: *Adoration of the Golden Calf.*
Illustration for Gnat Khotkevich's short story 'Aviron',
published in the journal Science and Religion, *February*
1968. It may be debated how far this drawing is anti-
religious at all

1920s. Others look further back to the unbroken tradition of Russian iconography, which itself was inherited from Byzantium. Neither trend is favoured by the official guardians of culture; yet it is difficult to see the future of Russian art in any other terms than a vying between the two for supremacy. Socialist realism, embodying the official dogma of moral improvement, comes nowhere.

The art of the vocational painter is one of the least-known aspects of present-day Russian culture; the 'religious stream' in it is less known than the abstract. Our selection does not claim to be representative, for we are limited to those artists whose work has been brought out of the Soviet Union, either in the original or in reproduction. We know the names of a handful of Moscow artists who see in the religious tradition an inspiration for the enrichment of their art. Because most cannot exhibit in their own country, we know only the merest fraction of their work; of those who paint in the provinces we know nothing. Yet what we have is enough to arouse the keenest expectation for the arrival of the time when the fruits of the Russian spirit can again become part of the world's legacy.

With two exceptions, every artist whose work is represented here is in some sense in conflict with the society in which he lives—this is not to imply that any one of them is a disloyal Soviet citizen, but rather that he offers a creative alternative to those ideas which are the officially accepted norms of that society. If history offers any precedent, they all have a greater chance of achieving distinction than any of the conformists whose works crowd out the numerous sponsored exhibitions of Soviet art.

The two exceptions are included deliberately to broaden the scope of this selection. Russian popular speech is peppered with Bible-based expressions, which not even the politicians can purge from their vocabulary. There are religious particles in the air the Soviet artist breathes, so even the most conformist of them can sometimes illustrate a biblical theme without being aware he is doing so. The intention of Y. V. Vuchetich, in the work we have illustrated, seems to be to fulfil the canons of socialist realism and the allusion to Isaiah's prophecy was possibly more obvious to the collective farm worker than the sculptor.

More important and interesting is the very special category of anti-religious art, more often created as a visual aid to atheist writing than to stand independently. The anti-religious cartoon is the most common expression of this, but its general standard is far too low to reproduce here. Just occasionally, however, the fine tradition of Russian graphic art comes into its own to produce a piece of genuine power.

For most of the remainder of Russian artists, the prospect of success and acceptance seems to have advanced only imperceptibly since the dethronement of Stalin. In 1962 Khrushchev behaved with almost unbelievable coarseness at an exhibition of works by Moscow artists, which was immediately closed down. In 1966 the newspaper, *Soviet Culture*, called Oscar Rabin a 'truly miserable wretch' and the exhibition of his work the previous year in London was a 'provocation aimed against Soviet art'.

Unlike the less fortunate underground writers, they remain free men, yet their lives are beset at every turn with problems quite different from those of their counterparts in the West.

There can be no free interplay of ideas, either through exhibitions or discussion of principles in art journals. If they wish to make a living from painting, they must prostitute their integrity to adopt a second style of socialist realism, or they must find work as restorers of frescoes in ancient churches. It is not surprising, then, to find them still striving to establish a style, experimenting to discover how far the tradition of old Russian iconography can be stretched in a valid expression of new ideals. As with many other young people, allegiance to traditional Church dogma is weak, but the attraction of Christian spirituality is strong. The artists may outrun Church leaders in establishing contact with the disposition of the age.

Modern Church architecture is entirely unrepresented in our selection, for there is none in Russia. Yet if genuine freedom of religion should be established in the future, the situation will change at once. Thousands of towns and villages, at present without religious buildings or having only a shack adapted for worship, will offer unlimited scope to hundreds of architects and craftsmen. Russia could yet witness the twentieth century's greatest challenge to the Christian artist.

4 OSKAR RABIN (*born 1928*): *Charcoal sketch, 1963. Symbols of the Holy Communion (bread, wine, fish) against a modern Russian setting with reflection of a monastery. Exhibited London, 1965*

5 ILYA GLAZUNOV: St Sergius of Radonezh. *Oils. The greatest and most popular saint of the Russian Orthodox Church. Exhibited Rome, 1963*

6 DMITRI PLAVINSKY (*born 1937*): Pskov. *Pastel drawing before 1962. Study of a cross in a graveyard at Pskov, with Old Church Slavonic inscriptions*

7 ILYA GLAZUNOV: Mother of a Hero (*1962*). *Charcoal drawing. Fireworks in the sky symbolize victory but the mother stands at her Golgotha, looking at the photograph of her son, who will not come back. Exhibited Rome, 1963*

8 OSKAR RABIN: *Oils, 1965. Modern versions of traditional symbols (illuminated window, electric light, fish, wine) all enclosed in an egg, representing the Resurrection, surmounting a deserted church. The artist's whimsy (which underlines rather than calls in question his sincerity) is shown in the vodka bottle label indicating the alcoholic content and the cats on the church roof. Exhibited London, 1965*

9 DMITRI PLAVINSKY: *Charcoal and pastel drawing, 1962. Illustration of the resurrection to eternal life; a city rises from a graveyard*

9

10 ILYA GLAZUNOV (*born 1934*): The Brothers Karamazov (*1959*). *Pencil drawing inspired by Dostoevsky's novel. Forty works by this Moscow artist were exhibited in Rome in 1963. Most were on religious themes*

11 YURI TITOV (*born 1929*): The Golden Christ (*1964*). *Oils. This young Moscow artist first painted abstracts, then impressionist works, before 1963, since when he has devoted himself entirely to religious painting. Exhibited Bergen, 1967*

12 YURI TITOV: Alpha and Omega (*1965*). *Oils. One of a number of pictures by this artist in which he returns to the traditional iconographic style. The inscription '2 × 2 = 5' is probably a reference to Dostoevsky, who used the formula in* Notes from the Underground, *stating that irrationalism is preferable to logic*

10

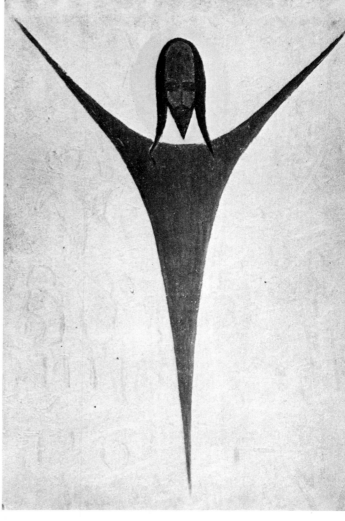

13 YURI TITOV: Destruction of
the Holy (*1967*). *Oils. One of a
series of dramatic representations
of the attempted destruction of
Russia's cultural and religious
heritage. In all of them the face of
Christ remains inviolate*

14–18 YURI TITOV: Five
Studies of Christ.

14 *Golgotha*
15 *Blood of Russia*
16 *Life of Christ*
17 *Destruction of the Holy*
18 *Conflagration*

203

19 MAXIM ARKHANGELSKY (*born 1929*):
Monk (*1963*). *Wood. This sculptor has
specialized in adapting the natural shapes
of roots and branches into artistic forms*

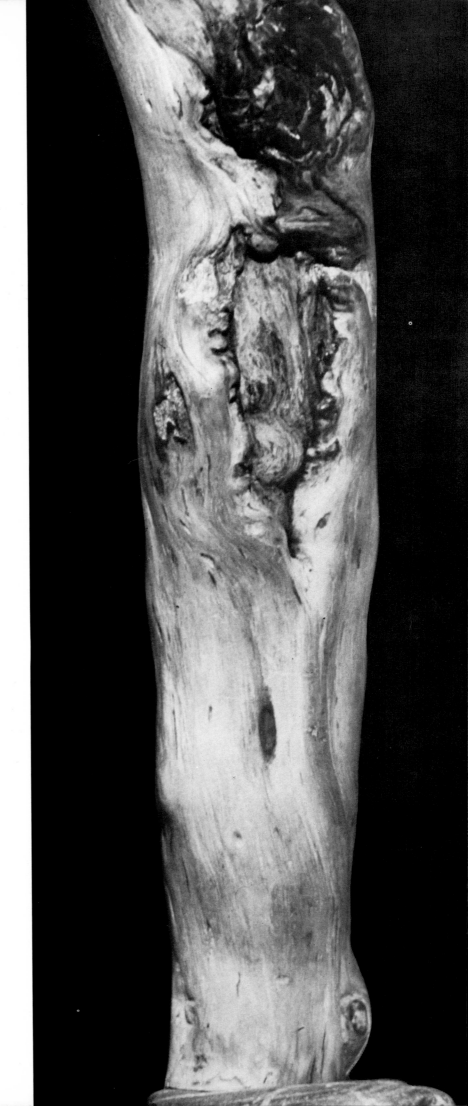

ROBERT SEFTON

THE CHURCH IN NORTH AMERICA

One of America's most esteemed historians has said that the clipper ships built on the Atlantic coast in the early 1850s were 'the most beautiful creations of man in America'. The assertion that only in the form of architecture is there an important statement of the way the people of North America have used art to express their relationship to God may be considered to be as subjective as Admiral Morrison's statement. But with the exception of a few examples of religiously orientated folk art; the work of the painter Edward Hicks in his innumerable 'Peaceable Kingdoms'; some Pennsylvania Dutch fracture painting; home-crafted metalwork as the Gabriel weathervane; there is little, aside from architecture, to suggest the concern for religious freedom (if only one's own) and the dependence on God that gripped the people of North America from the time of the early settlements to the end of the nineteenth century.

It is not surprising that the early colonizers when they approached the task of building their houses of worship chose to build them on the models of the 'old country'.

The English Establishment—Episcopalian, Church of England, centred on Virginia; the English separatists, Congregationalists, in New England; between them, in the mid-Atlantic states, a multitude of Protestant sects, Germans, Dutch, Swedish, predominently Presbyterian. There were the Spanish Catholics in the South-west and the French Catholics in Canada and the Gulf Coast areas. A rich diversity of faiths to say the least.

Each of these faiths produced houses of worship that were unique and individual, specially related to their country of origin but modified and transformed by the characteristics of their creed and the limitations of their locality.

The oldest existing church in North America is St Luke's, Smithfield, Virginia, built in 1632. A clear-cut facsimile importation, it is a typical example of the country churches then widely established in eastern England, with the massive square tower, the buttresses, the stepped gable, the double lancet windows, the quoins, the timber trusses and the great chancel window. This approach was not only limited to the Episcopalians in Virginia. We see it throughout the early settlements. We see

it in the sketch of the early Dutch Reformed Church built about 1690 in New Utrecht (now a part of Brooklyn, N.Y.). This small, charming, octagonal church with its steeply pitched roof might just as easily have appeared in Utrecht, Holland, as in New Utrecht, N.Y.

The New England meeting house is the exception to this rule of the European prototypes. Built by the democratically orientated Congregationalists of dissent and separation, these wooden structures served the dual function of a secular and a religious meeting place. (The first Plymouth Meeting House served also as a fort.) The Dissenters wanted their houses of worship to be deliberately ascetic and simple and not to contain any of the elaborate ritualistic trappings of the Establishment which they had abandoned across the Atlantic. Anything tainted with the liturgy or ritual of the Anglican Church was vigorously eschewed. The 'Old Ship' Meeting House in Hingham, Massachusetts (1681) is the only remaining seventeenth-century religious building in New England. Prim, proper, spare—these are the qualities that typify the Puritan plain style and are found in this interesting building. Square in plan, boxy in proportions, this clapboard meeting house with its simple fenestration does not suggest that its designers had looked to Europe for their inspiration. The 'Old Ship' appellation is suggested by the curved timbers and knee bracing supporting the hipped roof which, if viewed upside-down, resembles the interior of the hull of a ship; the use of the compass rose as decorative motif in the pulpit and belfry, and the captain's walk on the roof. All suggest that this church was built by ships' carpenters for men of the sea. Note the austerity of the interior: the plain plaster walls, the natural finished wood. There is nothing to distract from the emphasis upon the pulpit which is the only decorative element in the whole space, and even this has received very austere treatment.

Diversity is clearly the characteristic that can best be applied to this period of early church building in North America. A dramatic contrast to illustrate this climate of diversity is found in a study of two houses of worship. Though built only forty-three years apart these two buildings could not be more contrasted. One is absolutely artless in the austerity of its message; the other marshals all forms of artistic expression to create a special mood of mystical stimulation. The Friends' Meeting House, Locust Valley, New York, built in 1725, is typical of so many Quaker houses of worship. Simple wood frame, shingled exterior, covered porch at one side, residential in scale, it is unassuming, quiet, passive. It seems to express so well the simple, non-authoritarian, introspective faith of the Friends. The interior is furnished only with the barest of simple wooden pews. There is no altar, no pulpit, no choir, no music, no

1 *The Crucifixion; fractur watercolour by an unknown artist. Williamsburg, Virginia*

2 *Gabriel weathervane, Williamsburg, Virginia*

3 *Sketch of the Dutch Reform Chapel, Brooklyn, N.Y.*

cushions, nothing worldly to distract from a *vis-à-vis* communion with God.

In contrast, the Mission Church of San José y San Miguel de Aguayo, San Antonio, Texas (1768) is full of emotional stimuli. Like so many other missions built throughout the South-west, this mission is an elaborate complex of church and cloister, residential, storage and service buildings. These missions were self-contained oases of culture in the wilderness. Though elaborately laid out like European medieval monasteries, they also express the simplicity of those who actually built them. They reflect in this duality the social structure of the Spanish colonies in North America.

Dissimilar to that of the Atlantic seaboard colonies, which were tending toward a democratic society, the Spanish structure was built on more feudal lines. There were the masters—the Spaniards; and the slaves—the Indians. This polarity informs all aspects of this mission. The plan is elaborately Spanish. The materials (rough, tufa masonry), the simple geometric forms are Indian. The treatment of space, the accents of Baroque decoration are Spanish, the primitive manner of their execution Indian. The total effect is one of richness and high-keyed spirituality, a compatible background for the ritual pomp and Baroque liturgy of the Spanish Catholic Church.

The eighteenth century fostered the growth of a new homogeneity in expression. American society, through growing widely, was beginning to broaden at the base, to stabilize. People were beginning to think of themselves as Americans rather than Swedes or Dutch or English, or as Congregationalists, Lutherans, or Catholics, and were beginning to acquire characteristics (not all revolutionary) in common. The colonies as a whole were becoming more homogeneous politically, socially and, from the evidence of their church art, spiritually too. Improved means of communication between the colonies was one reason for this. Another was that the gradual emergence of England as the dominating major foreign influence tended to knit the diverse communities together.

The influence of English architecture, especially that of Sir Christopher Wren and his London churches after the Great Fire of 1666, had a strong impact throughout the country irrespective of creed, ranging widely from South Carolina through New England. The reasons for the predominance of the English style are many: one certainly is the success of some of the early examples which adapted so naturally to American soil. Bruton Parish Church in Williamsburg (1711) beautifully exemplifies this suitability: the natural-coloured brick, simply but decoratively detailed, the plain forms of the carpenter-crafted steeple, the slight Georgian detailing at the eaves and in the round-headed windows. All the elements seen here as

mere suggestions were to serve as the themes for an infinite number of variations.

It was during the 1720s that the full impact of Wren's work began to be felt in America. This influence was to have a profound effect on all church building to the present day, and has transcended the divergencies of creed, the exigencies of locality and the limitations of materials. The style of Wren and of his countryman, James Gibbs (though neither actually designed one church in this country), spread throughout the colonies. It was disseminated partly by their students and disciples who worked in America, more so through their books of architectural examples. Lacking local architectural talent, it was customary for carpenter-builders to take their inspiration, their proportions, and their detailing from these published examples. The First Baptist Church, Providence, Rhode Island (the congregation founded by Roger Williams), takes its steeple from St Martin-in-the-Fields, London, and the main body of the building from Marylebone Chapel, shown by James Gibbs in his *Book of Architecture* (1728).

This book is also credited with St Michael's Anglican Church (1752) in Charleston, South Carolina. Another popular book, *The Country Builder's Assistant*, by Asher Benjamine, details the plans, sections, elevations and even the pulpit details found in the Congregational Church (1806) in Bennington, Vermont. There is careful adherence to the Palladian details in this obviously carpenter-built church. This Congregational Church is, in its elegance, delicate detail and spatial composition, a far cry from 'Old Ship'.

Further removed still from 'Old Ship' is Center Church in New Haven (1814), also Congregational, designed by Ithiel Town from plans purchased from Asher Benjamine. This church is one of the great city churches of the period. Extremely elaborate detailing in brick and wood has produced a sophisticated and urbane monument which better reflects the social and economic status of the congregation than its spirituality or credo.

Unquestionably the high point in the art of the Christian Church in North America is King's Chapel, Boston (1754). Peter Harrison, so-called first American architect, was the designer of this beautiful Anglican church. Although the steeple has never been completed, giving the exterior a rather chopped-off stumpy look, the interior is a masterpiece of sensitive design. It has a grandeur of scale and a plasticity of form of the highest calibre. It has a graceful beauty in the fine carved Georgian details, in the Corinthian columns and capitals, the Palladian window, the balustraded altar-rail, the finely proportioned panelling. Note how the column bases are raised above the pew level so that the effective rhythm of the unusual paired columns

4, 5 *Exterior of St Luke's Church, Smithfield, Virginia, the oldest church in North America, built 1632*

6, 7 *Exterior and interior, the 'Old Ship' Meeting House, Hingham, Massachusetts*

is fully expressed. All these elements combine to create a calm, serene, truly beautiful church.

The prevailing rationalism of eighteenth-century America with its distrust of emotion in religion had created an atmosphere that nourished the elegant Classical style of Harrison. With the advent of the Romantic period in the mid-nineteenth century a change in this approach to religion began to develop and the role of emotion, feeling and the recognition of the place of the senses in things religious or spiritual, was re-established. This new attitude, in conjunction with the proliferation of the revival styles progressively in vogue throughout this period, has provided us with a widely varied finale to this study.

These examples, which may not be as stylistically immaculate as those seen so far, are interesting nevertheless in their variety and their individuality. Most popular of all the revival styles, for obvious reasons, was the Gothic. We see it in many manifestations: the large stone church such as Trinity in New York, a rural wooden chapel in Canada, and in the great Temple of the Mormons in Salt Lake City.

Trinity is certainly the most true to the spirit of the historical prototypes and therefore a little dry and unexciting. But it is one of the most beautiful examples of a type that has spread throughout America in endless variations and sizes. Sharon Temple in Holland Landing, Ontario, built in 1825 by a splinter group of Quakers called the Children of Peace, is suggestively Gothic rather than architecturally so. It is said that every form and proportion in this building had a particular sacred significance. It has a certain doll's-house simplicity and scale which is quite charming.

Though separated in time and locality, in rituals and in beliefs, there is something of Sharon Temple lurking in the Mormon Temple, Salt Lake City, Utah. This edifice is one of the most imposing religious monuments of North America, not so much in its aesthetic appeal as in its symbolic majesty. The Church of the Latter-day Saints is a native American sect, founded by Joseph Smith in western New York State in 1830. After a considerable period of violent opposition culminating in the murder of Smith, the Mormons were forced to seek a home in a wilderness that no one else wanted. They settled at Salt Lake City and in 1853 proceeded to build their temple. Forty years and four million dollars later their granite temple was complete. Since the day of its dedication it has not been open to the public. The Mormons think of their church as a temple in the ancient Hebrew sense, as a place not for worship and services but as a sacred precinct reserved for special 'ordinances' and ceremonies. The exterior of this building suggests one great soaring interior nave as in the great cathedrals of Europe. In reality the interior is a four-storeyed structure

containing a honeycomb of smaller spaces for various ceremonies that are decorated in a particularly dated Victorian fashion typical of many Mormon temples of this period, such as the temple of Manti, Utah. Only on the top storey is there a congregating space and this gives the appearance of being quite modest in comparison with the monumental exterior.

Probably the most individual and singular church in America built before the twentieth century is the Whalers' Church in Sag Harbor, N.Y. Sag Harbor, along with New Bedford, Salem and Nantucket, was one of the great whaling ports of the mid-nineteenth century. This church, built in the 1840s, was designed by Minard Lefever, a self-taught architect. Although it has some decorative details derived from whaling such as the parapet ornament of blubber spades and the steeple in the form of a mariner's spyglass, and although built by artisans skilled in the craft of shipbuilding, the remarkable fact is that this church is in the style of Egyptian Revival. The forms of the exterior, the battered walls, strong horizontal parapets, interior details such as the papyrus leaf capitals, canted doorways and the decorative swastika mouldings, all are out of Egypt. Why was this exotic style selected for this place and use? Certainly not because whaling and whalers are particularly identified with Egypt. It has been suggested that Freemasonry, then popular with the wealthy ship-owners, with its strong dependence on Egyptian symbols and forms, was the factor that influenced this choice.

In the three-century span that has been under consideration in this study of the art of the Christian Church in America, we have seen the pendulum swinging from diversity to homogeneity and back to diversity yet always potently influenced by the culture of Europe. It is really not until the twentieth century that the church in America was able to express itself in a completely native and original vernacular.

9

10

12

11

8–11 *San José Mission, San Antonio, Texas. The Spanish-Catholic influence is very plain*

12 *Friends Meeting House, Locust Valley, N.Y.*

13, 14 *Exterior and interior, Bruton Parish Church, Williamsburg, Virginia*

13

14

15 *First Baptist Church,*
Providence, Rhode Island

16 *St Michael's Church,*
Charleston, South Carolina

17, 18 *Exterior and interior, Congregational Church, Bennington, Vermont*

19, 20 *Interior of King's Chapel, Boston, Massachusetts*

17

18

19

20

21 *Detail of pulpit of King's Chapel, Boston, Massachusetts*

22 *Exterior of Temple of Church of Jesus Christ of Latter-day Saints—the Mormons—Salt Lake City, Utah*

22

23 *Interior of Sealing Room for the Living, Mormon Temple, Manti, Utah*

24, 25 *Detail and general view of the First Presbyterian Church, Sag Harbor, N.Y.*

26 *Before the hurricane of 1938 the church had a steeple*

26

27

27 *Modern church in Naples, south-west Florida*

28 (overleaf) *Trinity Church, New York*

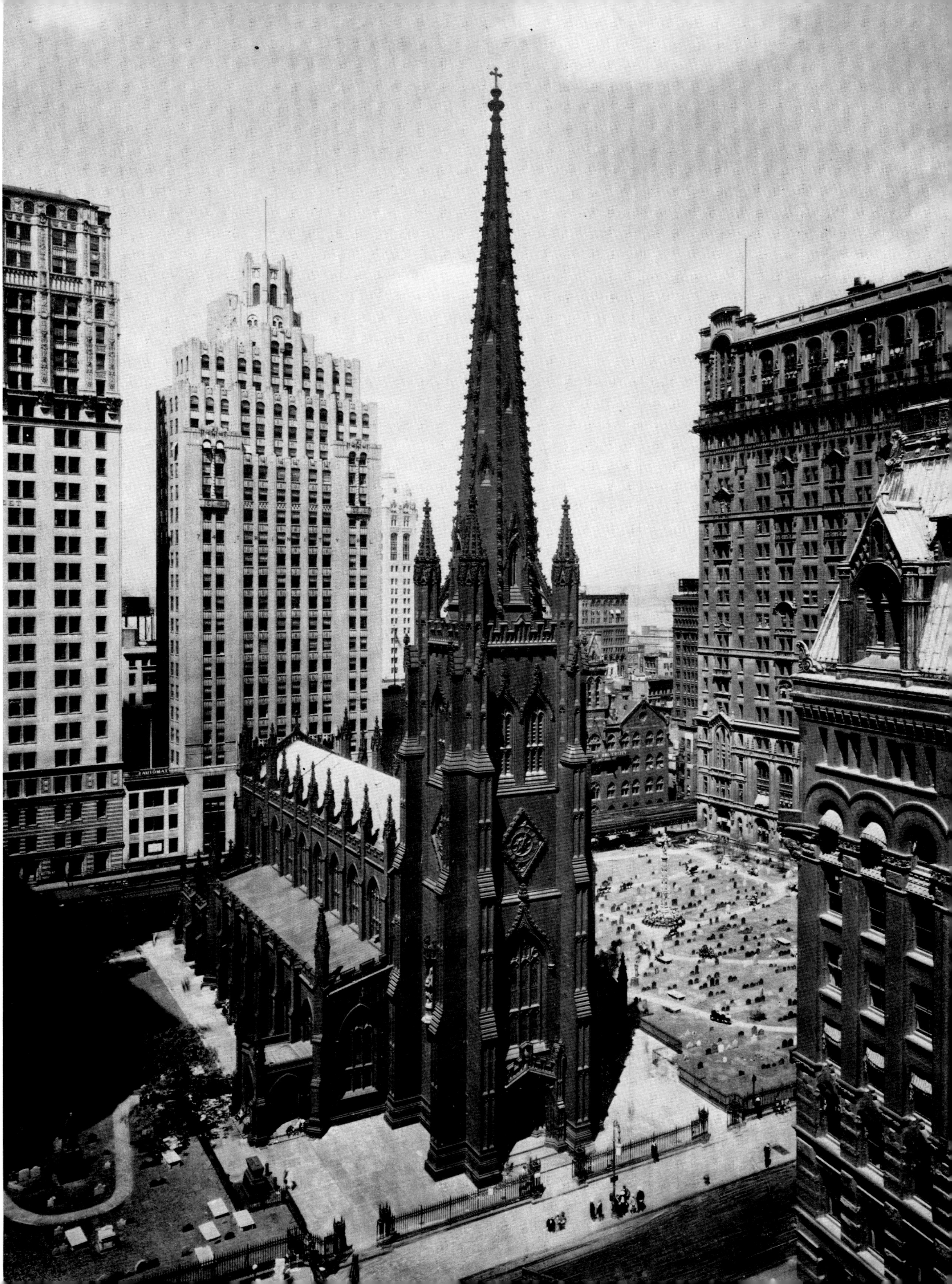

COTTIE A. BURLAND

THE CHURCH IN SOUTH AMERICA

The first contacts between Christians and the American Indians of Latin America developed from the voyages of Christopher Columbus, who made his first landfall in 1492. All the artistic influences stemming from Europe were conditioned by the High Renaissance, which later was to develop into brilliant versions of Plateresque, Baroque and Rococo, even into the irrepressible gaiety of Churrigueresque. Certain Spanish churches in Mexico and New Mexico have an echo of Gothic tradition, but this arose from the possibility that they might have to be used as fortresses. Hence high walls, narrow windows, and semi-defensive machicolations around the parapets. In every way local styles were conditioned by fashion within the Habsburg dominions in Europe. Sometimes one notices a closer comparison with the Baroque in Austria than with the Spanish version. Perhaps the influence of Portuguese traditions in the older cities of Brazil gave a special flavour, almost a simplicity, when compared with the brilliance and excitement of ecclesiastical art in the Spanish Colonial area.

There is a very definite American-Indian influence to be noted in selected regions, especially in decorative arts of all kinds. This however comes only from the technically advanced peoples of Peru, Colombia and Mexico. The populations were already large and included well-trained technicians at the time of the Spanish Conquest. In these regions the employment of Indian labour and the education of Indian craftsmen in new techniques made possible a rapid and brilliant development of ecclesiastical arts. Local participation was quite real, and the status of the craftsman removed him from the shadow of slavery. The Indian contribution was unique, differing in detail in each region. From Peru we have competent stone-carving with a tendency to massive forms, for silver and wood-work to take on repetitive pattern, and for vestments to include colour change in a rather specially Indian taste. From Colombia minor works of art have a tendency to more elegance of pattern, and metalwork is finished to a very high degree especially where native methods of surface gilding were used. Mexico contributed splendid vestments decorated with pictures in humming-bird feathers, and carvings which incorporate Indian

221

symbols for stars, flowers and plants, once the insignia of ancient gods.

In religious painting we have deliberate efforts by the local artists to adapt to the artistic tradition they observed from the paintings imported from Europe. They also produced in all regions delightful ex-voto paintings rather reminiscent of similar developments in European peasant art. There remained no room in their minds for the development of themes from their own past. In fact the past had come to such a violent end that they could only see it as unworthy in comparison with the arts which they learned in the workshops of their new masters. Many schools taught artists in Latin America, not for the development of design but for the reproduction of accepted European works. The training was very thorough and effective. In Mexico in particular the school founded for the children of Aztec nobility in Santiago Tlaltelolco created a specifically Mexican–Spanish style which was a very successful hybridization.

In all accounts of the progress of Indian craftsmen after the Spanish Conquest we hear of the jealousy of Spanish craftsmen who found their apprentices were outstripping them and consequently obtaining favourable prices for their work. This applied fully to ecclesiastical art. The beautiful things were produced commercially and purchased for the churches by benefactors who seem to have exercised rather particular good taste. The Spanish and Portuguese possessions were distinguished by an art which was perhaps to be described as provincial in many areas, but in the greater cities it was fully equal to the contemporary products of Europe.

Development through time followed the fashions of Europe, but in all Spanish America there was an added exuberance a little earlier in time. The immense wealth which accrued to the colonists from the mines of silver and gold, and from the emerald mines, allowed an exuberance which is hardly believable. The Incas may have ringed their chief temple with a cornice of solid gold, but in the richer mining areas, golden Rococo altars, and even entire reredoses in gold sheet beaten in high relief were made. Both colonists and Indians accepted the ecstatic nature of Catholicism. They received visions and commemorated them in paintings and statues. They rejoiced at Christmas and made the most wonderful Nativity shrines. They suffered at Easter with re-enactments of the Crucifixion carried on amid self-castigations almost beyond belief. Thus their Calvaries have a stark suffering which is not often found in Europe even at the height of the over-realistic Rococo. Although in architecture there had been a regular progression of style one notes that the minor arts in the service of religion were exuberant from the beginning. The Indian temperament, while

accepting the aspect of suffering in common with the 'Lutheran heretics', had no room for the sober solemnities which flowed from northern European sources. The consonance between the Spanish temperament and that of the Indians is marked.

In Brazil the whole matter had a different balance. The country was wild and, at first, poor. Gradually plantations with negro slaves became the main source of wealth. Trading cities grew more steadily, and the social structure of the country was far more liberal than the Spanish Colonies. As a consequence the development is never so rich and the architecture is often a fine Baroque with some very good sculpture. Lesser religious ornament and altar furniture tends to be somewhat more restrained. Small objects may show African rather than American Indian influences, and much influence can be traced from the Yoruba peoples of Nigeria who were traders visiting Brazil from time to time during Colonial days.

In effect the Church was part of the organization of State in Latin America, to the extent that the King of Portugal and the Emperor and later the Kings of Spain were the ultimate authorities in all civil matters whose judgement was invoked by the Vatican in appointing the bishops and senior clergy. This all tended to produce a uniformity at the top. In the many monasteries and nunneries works of charity were conducted within the orbit of the Establishment. However, these institutions were great patrons of the arts and not only vied with one another in the beauty of their churches, but glorified their buildings with ecclesiastical furniture of great richness, including paintings by the best available masters. It did not help the development of indigenous art traditions because the tendency was for both Indians and Creoles to accept the European tradition as the perfect expression of art. The strange complacency which inspired art in Mannerist and later circles in Europe was fully echoed in the Americas. Even in Mexico the Indian inspiration gradually disappears and although we know of many great artists of Indian descent in seventeenth and eighteenth-century Mexico, their work is a faithful reflection of the styles of Spain.

The basic difference of inspiration is a typical Latin American gaiety and spirit of rejoicing. The Faith was not a matter for the exercise of respectability, and so it often burst forth in a blaze of decoration. Even the very proper viceregal society did not scorn elaborations of fashion far beyond the pretensions of the European styles. In their worship they liked to be surrounded by splendour and colour. It is true that the Colonies were ruthlessly exploited for their wealth; but this was repaid in part by the lavishness with which ceremonial and religion were patronized. The keynote was colour. It never attained to the precise and gentle elegance of even the extremes of Baroque in

2

1–3 *Every possible type of Spanish art finds emphasis in the church decoration of South America, from the restraint of this carved and decorated pulpit, through the tremendous glory of the high altar to the banality of the robed saint*

4 *The Virgin and the Fifteen Mysteries*

imperial Austria, but took the same process forward to its ultimate possibility. Hence a new beauty arises in Latin American religious art, which makes it an exciting variation on the themes of the old world. Even the beautiful tiled work of the Mudejar style in Mexico is cognate to Moorish Spain, but it has a new simplicity of outline and a strength of delineation which is not of the Old World.

In Colonial days there was oppression and brutality in the social world. Often one finds that Christian teaching was shamefully ignored where human rights were concerned. However, there was a different apolitical atmosphere which led to a spiritual equality of a kind now gone for ever. One finds that the folk-paintings, and the little clay shrines and images of the poor Indian peasantry, did not become separate from the richness of the churches where all classes could worship together—though of course in their proper social ranks within the building. Great wealth caused much greed, but within the community there was much goodness of heart and human helpfulness. Partly this depended on the absence of a power struggle when all power came from overseas. The Americas of the Colonial days were almost fossils of the feudal system dressed in the trappings of the Baroque. In this way we must look at their religious art, as something preserved in a unity during nearly three centuries of internal peace. The opulence and brilliance are expressions of human beings who found their most complete freedom in the services of a religion which was really felt to be more Divine than expedient.

1

5 *Feather mosaic picture of Christ from the sixteenth century*

6 *Convent of Cuilapan de Guerrero*

7, 8 *Detail from the roof of*
Santo Domingo, Oaxaco

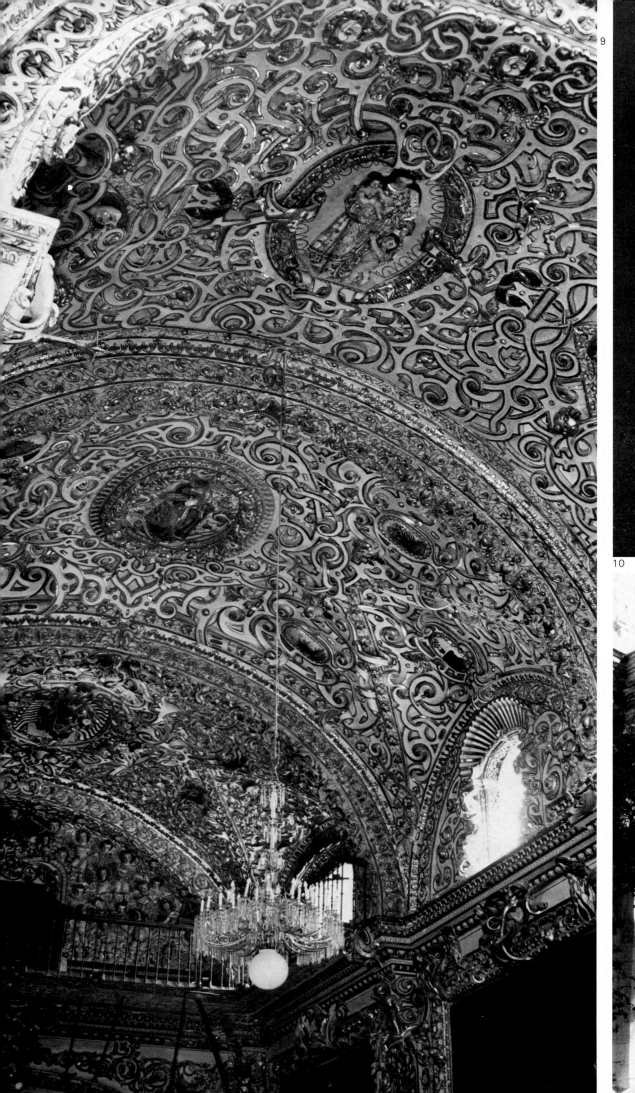

8

9 *Chapel of the Rosary, Santo Domingo, Puebla*

10 *Seventeenth-century monstrance*

11 *The cool, shaded interior of this church promises peace from the harshness of the outside world*

12

12 *Pulpit at Huaepiechula; its crude deep carving is in marked contrast to the low-relief pulpit in (1)*

13 *There is little comfort in this crucifixion, but for all the agony of the body the holiness of the spirit is revealed in the carving*

13

16

15

14 *Portrait of Christ*

15 *St Christopher, patron saint of travellers, carries the Christ Child on His journey*

16 *Stucco picture, probably the stoning of St Stephen or St Paul, on the wall of the church at Tlaxcala*

17 *Yangaitlan; the fan vaulting is Gothic, the apse High Baroque*

18 *Main door of the cathedral at Zacatecas*

19 *Wherever they went throughout the world the monks built
their monasteries and tended their vineyards*

20 *Tombstone near Vera Cruz*

20

21 *Madonna and Child*

22 *One of the plaster figures in Santo Domingo, Oaxaca*

23   24
25
26

23–25 *Interior and exterior of Santo Domingo, Oaxaca. The cool whiteness gives a sense of quiet which the ornate ceiling as shown in (7) and (8) disturbs*

26, 27 *The harshness of the land is all too clear; despite the church the vultures still flock to a carcass and emphasize the mortality of man*

27

28 *Church of Ocotlan, Tlaxca*

29 *Church in Taxco*

30

MARGARET HUBBARD

MISSION IN AFRICA

In the present century when the major cities throughout Africa are flooded by a wave of paintings and carvings known as 'Airport Art', specially produced to attract tourists by its primitive appearance, it is difficult to penetrate the disguise and discover true African art. The creations of the true African artist bear little or no resemblance to the curios produced on a commercial basis; the former bear the unmistakable stamp of the origin of the artist's inspiration and they are of exceptionally high craftsmanship. Carvings are remarkable for the powerful, rhythmic feeling for form, and the choice of grain of wood to accentuate that form. Paintings are outstanding for the imaginative and poetic use of colour, which, together with the wealth of detail drawn from the world in which the artist lives, produces dynamic pictures which magnetize the spectator.

The influence of Christianity manifests itself most plainly in the imaginative and narrative interpretation of Christian themes in the African idiom. Again and again this is to be discerned in the choice of subject-matter for carvings and paintings, as, for example, the numerous representations of scenes from the life of Christ and the many different approaches to the Madonna or Mother and Child theme. In all examples of this type of artistic creative work the strong imaginative sense and the rhythmic expression of form are present to a very marked degree. This gives these religious themes a power and glory of their own which speak movingly to the spectator and prove beyond doubt that the work is the creation of convinced Christian artists whose faith in God has orientated them.

This is the secret of the strength and greatness of the designs of the African artist. Elimo Njan, who was born in the foothills of Mount Kilimanjaro, is a gifted artist of strong Christian conviction and he interprets his thoughts and those of his fellow Christian artists in the following words: 'An artist without a faith is like a hoe without a handle—he can only scratch the surface.' Without faith it is impossible to penetrate to the heart of the matter. The true artist, who draws his inspiration from the community in which he lives, must accept and respond to the challenge presented by God. It is possible to discover this response in the work of many Tanzanian and West African artists who have created pictures and carvings full of spontaneous vigour. This has made African sculpture, in particular, a potent force in the contemporary art world.

Central Africa is known to be one of the least artistic parts of the continent as far as the fine arts are concerned, but to the Western eye many of the normal everyday articles of furniture such as cooking-pots, stools and so on have a magnificent sense of design and form which makes them particularly desirable. In the early days, when missions were first established, priests and mission workers were quick to notice the possibilities of these homely objects, and they soon adapted them for use as church furniture: there are good examples in Mapanza Mission Church, Zambia, where the prayer-stools are readily carved out of sections of tree trunks. Another example is the candlesticks on the altar at St John's Seminary, Lusaka; these were made by the natives of the Ba-Ila tribe, who are noted for their skill in carving articles from tree-trunk sections and are outstanding for the splendid simplicity and natural grace which is retained within the limits of the material. It is interesting to compare the Ba-Ila candlesticks with the Bemba candlestick now in the possession of the White Fathers. The former draw their strength from the simplicity of the design and the statuesque shape; in the latter is more delicate and flowing. From such plain stools as were in everyday use the Bemba people formed true inspiration for an African Christian altar. They placed planks across a stool and added a model of an African hut to form a tabernacle. This unaffected design has been developed and, as in the case of the high altar of Bujora, typical African patterns have been used as decoration; for example, the arrow, which is the symbol of love, has been used to indicate the penetration and depth of God's love for His people. In this way African craftsmen and artists have succeeded in producing decorative church furniture which is both functional and of high artistic merit.

The Church of the African Martyrs, Ndola, Zambia, has a large bark-cloth dorsal behind the altar. The bark cloth is beautifully decorated with crosses and lozenge shapes, which are repeated in a reticulated design reminiscent of a fishing-net. This amazing and probably unique piece of work was inspired when a priest observed an ancient African man repairing rents with decorative stitches which formed a design in themselves. There are some signs of wear—the dorsal is more than thirty years old—but it is still possible to appreciate the beauty of the design and the original choice of materials. In the same church the font is a wonderful example of the adaptation of genuine everyday articles for use as church furniture. An African pot, placed on a curved wooden pedestal, is the container for water, and wire delicately twisted round the neck of the pot has been fashioned into graceful candle-holders.

At the White Fathers Mission in Zambia, Father Corbert, who is an authority on African art, music and folk-lore, has several remarkable carvings by Africans in which it is possible to see the strong influence of Christianity. The most outstanding piece is a large wooden crucifix carved by a prisoner during his sentence at Broken Hill prison. The figure is majestic in its simplicity and economy of detail and yet the suffering of Christ on the cross is projected directly into the heart of the spectator. Also in the possession of the White Fathers is a magnificent set of vestments of African design, in which the arrow symbol reappears.

In the field of fine art, church decoration plays a major part. A chapel was built at Fort Hall near Nairobi, Kenya, in memory of the martyrs who were killed during the Mau Mau uprisings. Elimo Njan, a graduate of Makerere College and at present Director of Fine Arts, Nairobi, was commissioned to paint a series of significant events in the life of Christ on the chapel walls. In this series the artist interprets the theme in a way which suggests dignity through the imaginative use of colour and the typically African style of exaggerated human height in comparison to the world.

The churches in Africa led the way by commissioning artists and sculptors to combine their skills and to take their place in world art. Lamidi Fakeye carved a series of scenes from the life of Christ in bas-relief on the doors of the University Roman Catholic Chapel at Ibadan, thus helping to perpetuate the ancient African tradition of carved wooden doorways. The panel of the Annunciation, in which Mary is shown pounding in the traditional manner, is a particularly sensitive piece of carving; so also is the panel of the Wise Men bringing gifts. The church door at Cyrene, Rhodesia, carved by Sam Songo, is another excellent example. The panels in this door depict biblical scenes which are particularly connected with Africa, such as Moses stretching his rod over the Red Sea, interpreted here as an African watercourse, dry in winter but liable to swell to treacherous proportions in the rainy season. Cyrene is famous for the pictures of parables, saints and martyrs on the interior and exterior walls of the church, and also for the unusual style of drawing and painting which originated there under the guidance of Canon Paterson, the founder of the school. One of the best paintings is the 'Adoration of the Magi' on the exterior east wall, in which the Magi are dressed as Zulu chiefs to represent the local Matabele tribe who are descended from the Zulus of Natal. Other fine paintings on the exterior wall depict St Christopher, Noah giving thanks after the Flood and Mary Magdalen. Three promising Cyrene artists have recently completed a magnificent painting, in the African idiom, showing St Paul being shipwrecked at Malta. The fall of St Paul, which is skilfully painted, is full of character, and the whole composition compares favourably with the earlier murals. All the paintings are notable for the unusual use of

1–8 The Mission at Cyrene, Bulawayo, in Rhodesia, has been a centre for Christian art for many years and its pupils have travelled widely

1 Wood-carving of Moses summoning the waters of the Red Sea to engulf the host of Pharaoh

2 Crucifixion painted on the exterior wall of the church

colour and for the wealth of skilfully painted detail. The church is dedicated to the Martyrs and Missionaries of Africa and the sanctuary, which is a blaze of colour, is decorated with bold full-size figures of martyrs. These provide a strong contrast with the background of local scenery. The pictures are framed with simple geometric designs which are thought to have been inspired by ancient beadwork.

The influence of Cyrene has spread to other parts of Africa and there are some fine wall-paintings in the sanctuary of Chipili Mission Church, Zambia. These paintings, by Joseph Njamu who studied at Cyrene, include an excellent interpretation of Abraham, complete with hoe and knife, setting out to sacrifice his son. Unlike the glowing pictures at Cyrene these are subdued in colour, but in the composition and treatment of the subjects it is obvious that the artist found his inspiration at Cyrene. The Cyrene influence is also to be seen in an excellent crucifix in St John's Seminary, Lusaka, carved by the same artist, which compares favourably with the processional cross at Cyrene carved by Sam Songo, a more experienced sculptor. Also at Chipili, interesting examples of the development of graves under the influence of Christianity can be seen. The earliest examples are simple mounds of earth with nothing to mark them. As time went on graves were marked with the sign of the cross picked out with rough stones. Even later, *c*. 1934, a memorial stone to the Reverend Kasengula is thought to be of pure African design.

It is interesting to compare the original and dynamic art produced by Jesuit Father Engelbert Mveng of Cameroun with the highly imaginative work of Arthur Bucknor of Ghana, the naturalistic style of Job Mokgosi of Basutoland (particularly his painting of Shepherds going to visit the Holy Child) and the mystical and intellectual approach of Elimo Njan of Tanzania.

All these artists are working towards a common end, the tangible expression of their faith in God, showing that Christianity is a vital and living influence on the flourishing art of the African.

NOTO ENSIMINI·PFUMA MU MUNDA

ANDWA KUKA STEFAN·KURAIWA KWA STEFAN

6

7

8

9 *Copper crucifix of sixteenth or seventeenth century from the Kipangue Province of the Lower Congo*

10 *Head of Christ carved in wood in East Africa. The Arabic features and Assyrian beard are in sharp contrast with the Negro faces of the other side of the continent*

9

11 *'Behold my hands and feet'*

12 *Crucifixion; both paintings by Father Englebert Mveng, SJ, Cameroun*

13 *The Martyrs of Uganda. Detail from a composite mural of the twenty-two young men who were executed in 1886 by the King of Buganda, showing them in traditional bark-cloth toga and bearing symbols of their clan or court function*

14 *The altar at Bujora based on the concept of the chief's stool as a symbol of kingship, and an African hut*

11

12

13

14

17, 18 *Exterior and interior, Dodoma Cathedral, Tanzania*

19 *Mombasa Cathedral*

20 *All Saints Church, Kilembe Mines*

21 *Chapel at Wamumu Approved School*

22–25 *Series of murals depicting the life of Christ in a Kikuyuland setting, from the Church of the Martyrs, Fort Hall. The artist, Elimo Njau, can be seen at work*

23 *The Last Supper*

24 *The Baptism of Jesus*

25 *Gethsemane and the Crucifixion*

22

23

28

26 *Crib figures from Kamba, East Africa*

27 *Crib figures from the Oji River Leper Settlement, West Africa. These two sets of figures show the vast differences in style which pervade the continent*

28 *Calvary mural painted by a girl in Gayaza School Chapel, Uganda*

29 *'The Transfiguration', painted by Samuel Sempala, pupil at King's College, Budo*

29

30 *Bark-cloth dorsal at the Church of African Martyrs, Ndola*

31 *Crucifix carved by Joseph Njamu, candlesticks carved by tribesmen of the Ba-Ila, in the Chapel of St John's Seminary, Lusaka*

32 *Candlestick carved by a member of the Bemba tribe*

33, 34 *Carved pew end and prayer desk from Cyrene*

35 *Sculpture in wood showing the Holy Family. The heart-shaped face is one of the oldest and most widespread forms of African art*

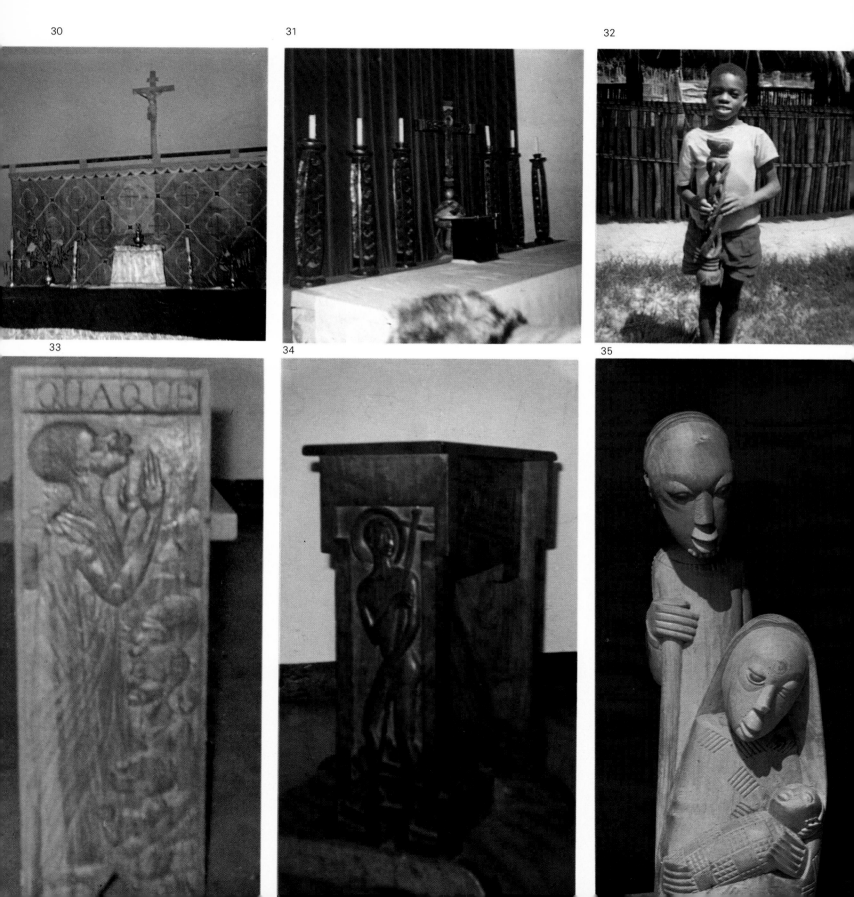

THE REV. DR JOHN F. BUTLER M.A.

INDIA AND THE FAR EAST

Hitherto in this book, Christianity has been treated as a religion of Europe, America, Africa, and just the Mediterranean fringe of Asia. Even the so-called 'Eastern' Churches have taken us no further east than a line formed by the Urals, the Caspian and the Jordan. Yet Christianity arose in Palestine, on the very easternmost fringe of the area so far considered. How can the art of Asian Christianity be left so late in an account of the art of a religion which began in Asia?

The answer lies in a set of historical facts. Firstly, Christianity, as has already been seen, became involved, very soon after its foundation, in the life of the Roman Empire; it shifted its centre to Rome, and its boundaries became much the same as those of the Roman Empire. Next, such tentative offshoots as Christianity had put out eastwards from Palestine were in the seventh century obliterated in the beginnings of that great out-surge of Islam which in the succeeding centuries all but overwhelmed Europe, being halted halfway up Spain only in the eighth century, and being still capable of capturing Constantinople, the Eastern capital of Christendom, in the mid-fifteenth century. Then, when Europe was able to push outward again, its west-facing sea-coast led it in America and Africa to fuller conquest than it ever achieved in Asia.

Yet throughout the Christian centuries Asia was under constant missionary pressure from Christendom, and one may distinguish four main phases of that pressure.

The first may be called, with rough accuracy, 'Nestorian'. During the first Christian millennium, small Churches in Syria and adjacent lands, some orthodox in theology, some unquestionably Nestorian, and some betwixt and between, spread eastwards, through the influence of their wandering merchants. It is probable that one such group of Near-Eastern merchants, landing about AD 400 in Travancore-Cochin, near the south-western edge of the Indian peninsula, were the actual founders of that ancient Church called the 'St Thomas Christians', which prefers itself to maintain that it was founded by the Apostle St Thomas, the Doubter, himself. This Church has survived through the centuries, despite Hindu pressures, internal dissensions, seventeenth-century struggles with and defections to Rome, nineteenth-century flirtations with Anglicanism, and the twentieth-century arising of a communist majority in the State; and today, in its two great 'Jacobite' and 'Mar Thoma' branches, it still has half a million members and is the main cause of the State of Kerala being one-third Christian in its population.

There is, alas, little remaining of the art of this, the most ancient Christian Church in Further Asia, from the period before the sixteenth century when Western models became decisive for church-building. There remain only a few, much-altered medieval churches, in a distinctively Travancore style; a few majestic outdoor crosses; and half a dozen indoor bas-relief crosses of about the ninth century, some bearing inscriptions in Pahlavi, old Persian. The finest and most famous of these, oddly enough, is not on the west coast at all, but by the Bay of Bengal, just outside Madras, in the Church of Great St Thomas's Mount, marking the reputed site of St Thomas's martyrdom. It has a reddish mark on its black stone, which local legend says is a stain of the Apostle-martyr's blood; it gave an astonishing series of miracles of sweating in the seventeenth century; and it is set in a lovely little sixteenth-century Portuguese church, under an icon which another local legend says was painted by St Luke, but which is actually quite old Byzantine work. What an epitome of church history that little cube of stone is!

Throughout the Dark Ages and the medieval centuries these 'Nestorian' merchants penetrated even further east. Their presence in the heart of China by 781 is testified by the dated inscription on the famous 'Nestorian Stone', with its fine carving in semi-Chinese style.

Somewhat similar, though later, in their origin are the Armenian churches, built along trade-routes by merchants of that wandering, because much-persecuted nation. The group of Armenian churches in Persian Julfa is well known; less so are the similar though less elaborate churches of about the seventeenth century in Madras and elsewhere in India, and the finely carved grave-slabs, all over south India, inscribed in the handsome Armenian script.

Apart from the 'Nestorian' wanderers, India and the Far East had few Western visitors in the early Middle Ages, though an emissary of our own King Alfred the Great is reported in the *Anglo-Saxon Chronicle* to have brought gifts to the reputed tomb of St Thomas in Madras. But later in the Middle Ages, when merchants like the Polo family were penetrating right through to the Far East, a whole series of adventurous monks, chiefly Franciscans, were doing the same, for the sake not of trade but of preaching. They saw little of India, because, like the Polos, they were intent on reaching the Court of the Great Khan himself. Nevertheless, four of them were martyred in 1391 at Thana, near Bombay, when on their way to a Franciscan bishop who had his see at Zaitun in China. By a strange chance,

in 1920–38 parts of the old walls of Zaitun were demolished, and several Christian tombstones of the fourteenth century were found, including one of an Italian bishop who died in 1392. They show a strange mixture of Islamic, Chinese and European styles.

These early contacts are of fascinating interest, but minor in scale. The third wave of Christian impact on Further Asia was a mighty one. By the end of the fifteenth century the Portuguese, and afterwards the Spaniards, were feeling their way down the west coast of Africa; they soon rounded the Cape of Good Hope; and in 1510 Goa was seized by the Portuguese and became the centre, politically, economically and ecclesiastically, of their great eastern empire. 'Factories' and governors were established all round India, on the coast of China and all over the western Pacific. On these journeys, as on the similar ones to Central and South America, the priests and friars were as numerous as the soldiers and merchants.

The innumerable churches and convents built by these men —often saintly and heroic men, especially in the first expeditions —were in full European style, for they were designed by European expatriates, men fully confident in their own faith and their own culture. At their best, these buildings were magnificent: Goa could rival Lisbon itself, and Macao any provincial Portuguese town, in glory of Baroque architecture. Only in a few details were there signs that these buildings were of the East; local materials, adaptation to the climate, the inbred techniques of the craftsmen, gave some little tincture of indigenous detail to the basically European designs. Much the same applies to the later, Protestant work of the Dutch and English who gradually displaced the Iberians—though with them there was even less indigenization, since their racialism was in most ways more pronounced and their sense of home ties was stronger.

However, even in this period of European euphoria there were some conscious attempts to make the Christian Church less of a foreign importation for its converts, less of a Westernization agency, and more a Christianizing of them as Indians, or Chinese, or men of whatever nation they were. Such efforts were in part promoted by and expressed in Christian arts which were consciously intended to be indigenous. Such arts were not easy to found. The missionaries, even when well-meaning in this respect, were deeply imbued with Western preconceptions. The converts themselves were not only dazzled by the prestige of the newly known West, but were also understandably cautious about the use in their cult of forms of art closely akin to the forms of the old faiths which they had abjured. Such fears were not trivially grounded: Christians were safe with European forms of art, since these had evolved in the course of expressing

Christian ideas: but a Divine Being symbolized in Asian modes was bound to look like Siva, or Buddha, or a Confucian sage—and was that the right way to show Our Lord Jesus Christ, or His God and Father?

Nevertheless, in south India in the early seventeenth century, a great Jesuit, the Blessed Robert de Nobili, did attempt at Madura a mission to Brahmins, the external forms of which were completely Indian. Despite De Nobili's outstanding learning, heroism and sanctity, his mission died with him, and has left no visible traces. A somewhat similar though less ascetic mission at the Imperial Court at Agra, founded by another great Jesuit, the Blessed Rudolf Acquaviva, began in 1580 and contrived to live on, ever dwindling, till 1803. Its strategy was that of a cultural assault upon the centre of power. It has left only a few minor buildings; and a number of contemporary Mogul miniature-paintings show Christian themes, and partially Westernized techniques, which derive from the Jesuit Fathers' interest in the local arts and their use in evangelism of Dutch Christian engravings.

In Japan, a promising Church was founded in the mid-sixteenth century; but soon, by a persecution of unparalleled ferocity, it was stamped out or, in a few villages, driven underground. Naturally there are no architectural remains of a Church which came to such an end, except for a few cave-churches in remote places. But several paintings and carvings, of mixed Italian and Japanese style, survive from the first flowering; and there are even a number of relics of the persecution-period itself. Some of these are images made or used by the persecutors as *fumi-e*, 'stepping images', on which suspected Christians were required to trample as a test of their faith; others are *nando gami*, 'closet gods', disguised cult-objects such as a *netsuke* (ornamental button) which opened to show a Station of the Cross inside, or statues of Kuan-Yin (a Buddhist goddess) or of the Buddhist *Dharma* (Law), or plates and cups, marked with ambiguous crosses for Christian culture. The memory of these heroisms, combined with the traditional Japanese reverence for the dead, has led the revived Japanese Church of our own day to show in its art an extraordinary predilection for scenes of martyrdom.

The outstanding expression of this indigenizing mode of evangelism was the great Jesuit mission at Peking, which began in the sixteenth century and, though with lessening force, survived well into the nineteenth. Matteo Ricci and his colleagues and successors made themselves respected at a very suspicious Court by their prodigious learning and their whole-hearted adoption of Chinese social manners; they indeed made themselves almost indispensable by their mastery of that astronomy on which the theocratic system depended. Architecturally, they left great secular monuments in the semi-Chinese Summer Palace and Observatory, and minor ecclesiastical ones in some of their own churches. In painting, Brother Guiseppe Castiglione and his peers themselves both painted Christian themes in semi-Chinese style, and introduced chiaroscuro and perspective into Chinese painting. Most important of all, they influenced the designs of the great porcelain craft, and caused the production of many pieces of pottery with Christian pictures in semi-Chinese style—the so-called 'Jesuit pottery'. Altogether, they were responsible for a not insignificant episode in Chinese art—though perhaps it was not really more important than the corresponding craze for *chinoiserie* in contemporary Europe.

These great Catholic missionary movements gradually died down in the eighteenth and nineteenth centuries, as the Catholic Powers lost their earlier vitality. In the nineteenth century came the next great missionary wave towards Asia, beginning with the great Protestant missions, and with the Roman Church then coming to a new lease of missionary life.

This new missionary phase began as another outpouring of Western self-confidence, and so its art (such as it was) completely copied Western models. But soon it was caught up in the modern world, with a humbled West, jubilant emergent nationalisms in the East, political liberations, and the ecclesiastical corollary of new Churches independent of their Western founders. All this in turn has inevitably led to Christian expression in indigenous arts.

Even before political nationalisms came to a head, there were a few isolated precursors of this movement towards national Christian arts, notably in the Indo-Chinese Cathedral of Phat-Diem (1875–95), and the Anglican Memorial Church of All Saints, Peshawar (1883), which resembles a mosque. But the real revolution came when Celso Costantini went out as Archbishop and Papal Delegate to China in 1922, and immediately instructed his clergy to build no more except in Chinese style. A painter himself by early training, he formed a

a   b   c   d

S. Thomé.—Pen-sketch of the Old Cathedral before 1892.

a.=South porch.   c.=St. Thomas' tomb.
b.=Belfry.   d.=Presbytery in which St. F. Xavier lived in 1545.

2

2, 3 *The sixteenth-century Portuguese cathedral of St Thomé Madras, reputed to contain the tomb of St Thomas, and the Neo-gothic replacement*

4 (opposite) *Fourteenth-century Christian tombstone from Zaitun showing the cross with Buddhist lotus and Chinese-style clouds*

3

group of non-Christian Chinese painters and set them to work on Christian themes in their own styles—and incidentally he baptized many of them before long. Back in Rome as Secretary of Propaganda and Cardinal he organized the Vatican Exhibition of 1950, which set the seal of official approval on indigenous art on the mission field. There is now a stream of such art, both Catholic and Protestant.

The dangers in such a policy, already mentioned, still remain. Aesthetically, it is only too easy to produce mere hybrids, flaccid arts without the strength of either local or Western tradition, and too self-conscious about 'style' to have force left for real creation. Theologically, the functions of a church are not the same as those of a temple or a mosque, and can be fatally disguised under forms borrowed from the buildings of other faiths; and the nature of the Christian Godhead may be given a distorted expression if forms are used which were devised to represent other theologies. Traps lurk in strange places. The story is told of a Chinese Christian schoolgirl, not well versed in her own country's art, who was distressed at a nationalist school-fellow's criticism of the Christian Church as un-Chinese. She therefore took the first opportunity of taking her friend to a Christian service conducted by a priest who, though a Westerner, was an indigenizing reformer, and wore Chinese symbols to adorn his vestments. That, thought the girl, would surely quench her friend's objections. On the contrary, it kept her doubled up with laughter throughout the service. She knew, as neither her Christian friend nor the priest knew, that the symbol on the vestment's right side proclaimed its wearer a bride, and on the left side an imperial concubine.

Life does not stand still. Crusades for indigenous Christian art may have meant much when Asian countries identified their national self-respect with the use of their national styles in art. But what now, when Le Corbusier has built a new Indian provincial capital in a style traditional neither to India nor to the West, but in the 'international style' of functional ferro-concrete? A Christ looking like Buddha may have appealed in Burma when the alternative was a Christ looking like a Western Renaissance male model; but will this help in the age of 'abstract' art? Western Christian art is in a hopeful ferment about its aspect of this problem; and so is the Christian art of Asia with its aspect of the same problem.

5, 6 Carved granite stone in St Thomé, Madras, dating from AD 600. One figure is St Thomas, the other either King Gondophores or another carving of St Thomas. This stone is sometimes incorrectly referred to as the 'Nestorian Stone'

8

7, 8 *Fourteenth-century tombstone of Catherine of Viglione, Genoa, who is buried at Yang-Chai, recalling the martyrdom of St Catherine of Alexandria, which is also depicted in the murals of Pickering Church, Yorkshire*

259

9 *Jesuit Church of Bom Jèsus, Old Goa (1594–1605). Now almost overgrown with palm trees, it was until recently the focus of a vast annual pilgrimage to the mummified body of St Francis Xavier*

10 *Tejgaon Church, near Dacca, East Bengal, is one of the few Portuguese churches to show any considerable measure of indigenization; the Baroque façade has marked Bengali features*

11 *Silver plaque from the coffin of St Francis Xavier, showing the miracle of the crab restoring the saint's lost crucifix. A series of such plaques was wrought by Goanese craftsmen for the coffin in 1636–7; sixty years later the coffin was set in a mausoleum sent out by the Grand Duke of Tuscany*

12 *Indo-Portuguese ivory of the Good Shepherd. This piece shows the classic Christian conception of the Good Shepherd and in the halo has God the Father blessing His Son; but the setting of the figure in a tree comes from one of the saucier legends of the Hindu God Krisna and below is shown another Hindu God, Visnu, in the sleep during which he is held to give the world its dream existence*

13 *Mogul miniature of the Virgin and Child—note the European dress of the attendants*

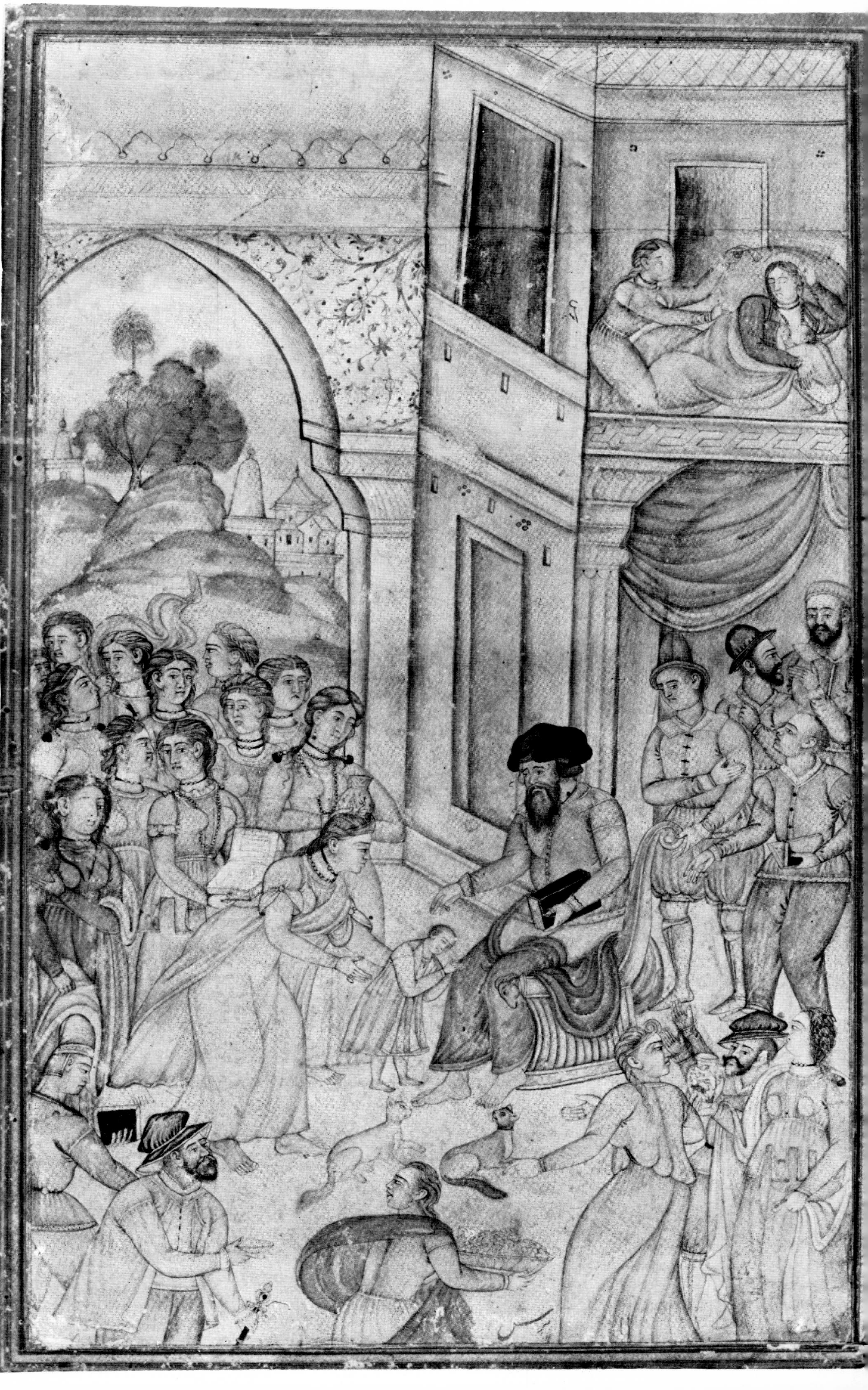

14 *Mogul miniature of the Presentation in the Temple. In this picture the main characters are in Portuguese dress, the attendants in Indian*

15 *The Last Supper (or perhaps the Marriage Feast at Cana). This picture was much influenced by contemporary Portuguese feasts in India*

16 *Teacup marked for secret Christian use, made in the sixteenth century in Japan during the period of the Great Persecution*

17 *Madonna and Child in the guise of the Buddhist Goddess Kwannon*

16

17

18 *Apparently a Mog*
impression of the Mass
though among other odd
the Virgin and Child ar
the altar and two of the
bystanders have the Mo
form of halo

19 *Chinese cup and plate with Crucifixion, painted about 1730 and known as 'Jesuit pottery'*

20 *Late eighteenth-century Indian-painted cotton picture of the Crucifixion*

21 *Tirupattur, Ashram; a Protestant chapel in an entirely Hindu style of building*

22 *Chapel and garden, Medical College, Vellore*

23 *A mandapam at Karachi. Mandapams, or open buildings, were erected in Hindu temples for various purposes; this was made as a resting-place for the idol when out on procession. Here European elements have influenced the design*

24, 25 *The Chapel, Bentinck Girls' High School, Vepery, built in the style of a mandapam*

26 *Detail of the tower at Tirupattur, Ashram*

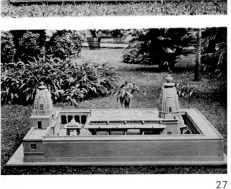

27 *Maquette for a South Indian Church. A great modern missionary, the late Father H. Heras, SJ, combined all the elements of the South Indian temple—the vimana (central shrine-tower), the mandapam (pillared hall or cloister) and also the less functional gopuram (gate-tower)—in this design. Although never built, the design has been very influential since being shown at the Vatican Missionary Exhibition in 1950*

28 *Seminary Chapel, Tumkur, Mysore. Originally Methodist, but now Church of South India, this chapel adapts the Indian shrine-tower type of building for Christian use*

29 Dornakal Cathedral. Designed by Bishop Azariah in a deliberate blend of Dravidian, Muslim and European styles to symbolize the Church's transcendence of race. It must surely be one of the most ungainly buildings in the world

30, 31 Interior and exterior. Church at Dudgaon, Hyderabad

32 Interior of the Chapel, Serampore College

33 Cathedral of Phat-Diem, 1875–95. Built by the Indo-Chinese convert known as 'Père Six' who was not only parish priest but also Viceroy!

34 Catholic Church at Pohsarang, east Java. This extraordinary building was designed just before the Second World War by a Dutch architect, Maclaine Dupont. The only wall, at the back, is non-structural; the roof is supported from non-rigid pillars acting like tent-poles and sways in the wind. Being flexible it is highly resistant to storm damage

35, 36 Exterior and interior of Catholic Church at Formosa

30

33

31

35

32

36

34

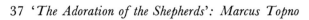

37 'The Adoration of the Shepherds': Marcus Topno

38 Madonna and Child from Bali

39 'The Nativity': Wajan Turun, Indonesia

40

*Indian and Chinese artists use both
their own and European idioms to tell
the Christian story*

41 42

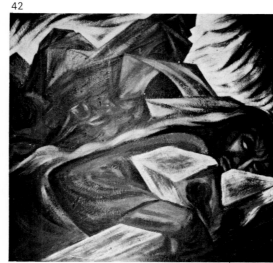

40 '*The Last Supper*': *Jamini
Roy*

41 '*The Last Supper*': *S. Chavda*

42 '*Jesus falls under the Cross*':
S. Gujral

43 '*Madonna and Child*': *Jaya
Appasamy*

44 '*The Presentation in the
Temple*': *Frank Wesley*

43

44

JAYA APPASAMY

45 '*The Annunciation*': *O. Rodriguez*

46 '*Mother of Peace*': *R. d'Silva*

47 '*Mary, Patroness of the Japanese Martyrs*', *silk
painting: Lukas Hasegawa*

48 '*The Flight into Egypt*': *Luke Ch'en*

49 '*Madonna and Child*': *Wu Song Tchang*

47

45

46

48

49

MARGARET HAINES

THE ISLANDS AND AUSTRALASIA

For many years after the coming of white men to Australia, the artistic skill of the aborigines, and the great beauty of much of their culture, were not fully appreciated.

When the first Englishmen arrived, late in the eighteenth century, the aborigines populated the whole Australian continent. Nomadic people, who lived by hunting and gathering natural foods, they moved from place to place within their own strictly defined tribal areas, following the seasonal abundance of game and plant food, building only the simplest of shelters from tree branches and bark. Living in the closest communion with Nature, both physically and spiritually, they were one with the birds and animals, the rocks and trees; part of the very land itself.

Their material possessions were few, as befitted their roaming life, consisting for the most part of weapons and food-gathering implements, simple containers, and highly secret and carefully hidden ceremonial objects. These were all made from the materials provided by the land around them—wood, bark, stones and feathers, shells and bones, and had little value in the eyes of the white settlers.

Their spiritual life, too, was centred in Nature and man's identification with it, in the creation of man and the natural features of the country by creator ancestors, and was expressed and taught in ceremonies, legends, paintings and carvings, songs and dances. The skill and mystical beauty of these forms of expression was lost on those who judged them by the current standards of European civilization, and they were regarded mainly as manifestations of savagery.

Maintained by strict laws and codes of conduct developed over the years to a pitch of complete suitability to the life and environment of the people, the aborigine's way of life soon crumbled under the tragedy of separation from tribal lands and the lack of understanding and appreciation of the white men.

With the wider vision and more sincere artistic values of this century, the fascinating and unique culture of the aborigines has come to be widely acclaimed; but this recognition has come almost too late. Today only a few aborigines in remote areas live just as their ancestors did, though in the northern and central parts of Australia many others, living on or in contact with missions and settlements, retain strong ties with their tribal traditions and are well versed in the ways of the 'old people'.

The art of the aborigines is closely bound up with their religious life and plays an important part in perpetuating their beliefs. Even when used for secular purposes, the designs are usually connected with the totems and myths which form such an integral part of the artist's existence.

Various forms of art have been practised. In some areas cave walls are covered with paintings of mythical beings, men and animals, while in others simple outline figures are engraved in rock surfaces. Weapons, implements and carved wooden figures are decorated with painted or incised geometric or linear patterns. For ceremonial occasions, intricate ground drawings, beautiful objects made from coloured feathers, and elaborate decoration of the body have all provided scope for the skill of the artists. However, the works which have brought most fame to aboriginal artists are the bark paintings of the Arnhem Land aborigines, in which they depict sacred stories, totemic animals and other designs in natural earth pigments on the inner surfaces of sheets of bark. This is still a living and developing art in Arnhem Land, and the artists have attained a high degree of skill in both technique and composition.

Christian missionaries working among aborigines were not able to benefit from any indigenous building style suitable for adaptation to their use, while the deep involvement of the art of the aborigines with their own religion made its use in Christian church decoration seem impossible. There was, therefore, no aboriginal influence on church design, decoration or art until recent years, though Church missions have for a considerable time been conscious of the importance of keeping alive for as long as possible the aborigines' own art. More recently, in areas where there are large concentrations of aborigines still influenced by ancestral traditions, successful attempts have been made to introduce the aborigines' own art into the decoration of the Christian churches, and further interesting projects of this nature are planned. Under the guidance of the Reverend G. Armstrong, Methodist Chaplain at the Government Welfare Settlement at Maningrida, aboriginal artists are painting Christian subjects in their own traditional style.

The life expectancy of aboriginal art in its purely tribal form is strictly limited. It is inevitable that as wider horizons open for young aborigines, they no longer have the same intense interest in tribal traditions. Any attempt to prolong the life of tribal art when the inspiration for it is gone could only lead to its decline. The careful introduction of sacred subjects outside aboriginal tradition, while the art is still vital, may prove to be the means whereby aboriginal art can retain its vigour and beauty as tribal motivation diminishes.

In the Territories of Papua and New Guinea the adaptation of the indigenous arts to Christian use has followed a somewhat different course from that in Australia. European settlement has been of shorter duration, dating from the middle of the nineteenth century, and Europeans still form only a small proportion of the population. The country itself is extremely rugged, precipitous mountain ranges covered with dense tropical jungle making communication by land difficult. The people live in village communities in the mountain valleys, or in the steamy heat of the coastal areas, and there is little or no contact between neighbouring groups. Some of the people in the highlands districts, when first contacted by Europeans, were unaware of the existence of other human beings outside their own community.

Agriculture is the mainstay of life. Crops of taro, sweet potato or bananas are cultivated, and this diet is supplemented by the hunting of wild pigs and small game, or, in the case of the coastal people, by fishing. Houses and communal buildings are constructed, utilizing the materials most readily available, such as coconut palm, sago or black palm. The buildings vary greatly from district to district, both in design and craftmanship, ranging from very simple structures to the elaborately decorated spirit houses of the Sepik River area.

Arts and crafts, too, are greatly affected by the restricted communication; there is a great diversity in art styles, in the amount and quality of artistic expression, and also in the degree to which this is expressive of the mythology and beliefs of the people. While in some areas there is a great wealth of art— intricate wood and bone-carving, exotic masks and ceremonial art—in other areas one or two arts or crafts, such as the making of tapa cloth or grass skirts, constitute the sole artistic expression of the people.

In contrast to the missionaries in Australia, the Christian missionaries in Papua and New Guinea have been able from their first arrival, to adapt the local building styles to their needs, and have utilized the inexpensive buildings wherever possible, coconut matting helping to furnish the simple interiors. In recent years the decorative arts of the people have been incorporated more and more into the design and furnishings of the churches. In each district this presents an individual problem to the church involved, and great ingenuity is shown in using local arts and crafts to obtain the maximum effect. Where possible, the indigenous decoration is chosen for its appropriate significance, but some of the designs, though having

1 *Interior of Church at Yirrkala, Arnhem Land, showing panels of traditional aboriginal painting. Several artists combined to paint these panels which depict important legends of ancestral beings. These paintings were placed in the church to symbolize the desire of the aboriginal people to live their lives in a Christian context*

some original traditional meaning, have been developed and used in a purely decorative manner, and are applied in this way to church decoration.

Most European Christian missionaries are very appreciative of the quality and importance of indigenous art, and discourage any deterioration of the artistic standards. Unfortunately many fine examples of church buildings and decoration in Papua and New Guinea no longer exist, as the materials used in their construction are not very durable in the humid climate.

Maori artists are making an important contribution to church decoration in New Zealand. The Maoris, Polynesian people who settled in New Zealand in the fourteenth century, had a great heritage of decorative art. After New Zealand came under British sovereignty in 1840, and Europeans settled throughout the Maori tribelands, arts and crafts were sadly depleted as the traditional way of life was disrupted and more and more people adapted themselves to European culture.

There are, however, a number of Maori craftsmen still skilled in the ancient arts and traditions, and their beautiful and intricate wood-carving, with its highly developed spiral and figure designs, and reed matting woven in traditional patterns, are being used with great effect and meaning both in church buildings and in Maori meeting houses, which are used for church services and social gatherings.

In New Zealand, as in Australia and New Guinea, the Christian church, by the use of indigenous arts, is not only helping to preserve ancient skills; it is at the same time drawing from them vitality and beauty, to the enrichment of church art.

2 *Stained glass window, Milingimbi Methodist Mission, Arnhem Land, depicting the cross in a setting of aboriginal totemic symbols. The window was made to a design by the Reverend E. A. Wells from colour photographs of clan symbols. Every part of the design is symbolic and has much meaning for the aboriginal people of the area*

3 *Nativity painting by Mick Magani of the Jinang tribe. Inside the cave Mary and Joseph are bending over the Baby Jesus. Also watching are some fellow tribesmen, some birds and a small kangaroo; some shrubs are growing close at hand. Outside the cave the wise men are travelling through rocky country to visit the child. Various types of trees and tubers (for food) are shown*

4 *Nativity painting by Bobby Baijjaray of the Maili tribe. The Baby Jesus can be seen on the paper-bark while Joseph and Mary in Mimi dress stand to the left. Hunters come with their dog to see the Child. Above, the Mimi angels are singing to the accompaniment of didgeridoo and clapsticks and one is announcing the good tidings. Their spears are laid in a bundle. A dreaming snake stands up; the black background and white spots on the left indicate night. Mimis are elongated 'stick' drawings of spirit figures occurring in certain parts of Arnhem Land*

5 *Nativity painting by Mick Magani. There is a double Nativity scene here showing Mary, Joseph and the Child Jesus in a rock shelter. Various types of trees stand nearby and small creatures have come near. Further away under the moon and stars a hunter is about to spear a big kangaroo. A goanna, wallaby and a small bird are in the bush there, too. Another man is holding aloft a ceremonial object, probably a 'morning star'*

6 *Nativity painting by Bilinyarra and Daingangan of Arnhem Land. In the bark shelter the artists have painted a number of babies wrapped in paper-bark and a man standing by with a spear in his hand. To the left are shepherds and a man in a high ceremonial hat and two stars. To the right are two people with various kinds of dilly-bag which are given as gifts. At the top of the painting is a large rock snake and a star*

3

4

5

6

7 Chapel at the Evangelists' College, Jigarata, Papua, built in the style of a Sepik Spirit House. The house, Tamberan, or Spirit House, in every Sepik village is used as a men's club-house and a place where sacred spirit figures are kept

7

8 'Our Lady of the Aborigines', Darwin Cathedral. Oil painting by Karol Kupka commissioned by Bishop O'Loughlin as a reminder that the message of Christianity is universal and to help bring religion to the people in terms of local understanding. The Holy Child is seated in typical aboriginal fashion on His Mother's shoulders. The background pattern is formed of totemic designs selected from bark paintings, cave drawings and artefacts

9 Church at Menapi built in the style of local houses using coconut leaves and bindoro posts; bindoro is a widely used hard wood. The interior has a floor of fine coral with coconut mats for kneeling. The altar frontal is made in the same way as the grass skirts of the area but dyed in different colours

MARGARET HAINES

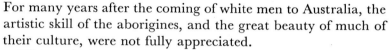

THE ISLANDS AND AUSTRALASIA

For many years after the coming of white men to Australia, the artistic skill of the aborigines, and the great beauty of much of their culture, were not fully appreciated.

When the first Englishmen arrived, late in the eighteenth century, the aborigines populated the whole Australian continent. Nomadic people, who lived by hunting and gathering natural foods, they moved from place to place within their own strictly defined tribal areas, following the seasonal abundance of game and plant food, building only the simplest of shelters from tree branches and bark. Living in the closest communion with Nature, both physically and spiritually, they were one with the birds and animals, the rocks and trees; part of the very land itself.

Their material possessions were few, as befitted their roaming life, consisting for the most part of weapons and food-gathering implements, simple containers, and highly secret and carefully hidden ceremonial objects. These were all made from the materials provided by the land around them—wood, bark, stones and feathers, shells and bones, and had little value in the eyes of the white settlers.

Their spiritual life, too, was centred in Nature and man's identification with it, in the creation of man and the natural features of the country by creator ancestors, and was expressed and taught in ceremonies, legends, paintings and carvings, songs and dances. The skill and mystical beauty of these forms of expression was lost on those who judged them by the current standards of European civilization, and they were regarded mainly as manifestations of savagery.

Maintained by strict laws and codes of conduct developed over the years to a pitch of complete suitability to the life and environment of the people, the aborigine's way of life soon crumbled under the tragedy of separation from tribal lands and the lack of understanding and appreciation of the white men.

With the wider vision and more sincere artistic values of this century, the fascinating and unique culture of the aborigines has come to be widely acclaimed; but this recognition has come almost too late. Today only a few aborigines in remote areas live just as their ancestors did, though in the northern and

273

central parts of Australia many others, living on or in contact with missions and settlements, retain strong ties with their tribal traditions and are well versed in the ways of the 'old people'.

The art of the aborigines is closely bound up with their religious life and plays an important part in perpetuating their beliefs. Even when used for secular purposes, the designs are usually connected with the totems and myths which form such an integral part of the artist's existence.

Various forms of art have been practised. In some areas cave walls are covered with paintings of mythical beings, men and animals, while in others simple outline figures are engraved in rock surfaces. Weapons, implements and carved wooden figures are decorated with painted or incised geometric or linear patterns. For ceremonial occasions, intricate ground drawings, beautiful objects made from coloured feathers, and elaborate decoration of the body have all provided scope for the skill of the artists. However, the works which have brought most fame to aboriginal artists are the bark paintings of the Arnhem Land aborigines, in which they depict sacred stories, totemic animals and other designs in natural earth pigments on the inner surfaces of sheets of bark. This is still a living and developing art in Arnhem Land, and the artists have attained a high degree of skill in both technique and composition.

Christian missionaries working among aborigines were not able to benefit from any indigenous building style suitable for adaptation to their use, while the deep involvement of the art of the aborigines with their own religion made its use in Christian church decoration seem impossible. There was, therefore, no aboriginal influence on church design, decoration or art until recent years, though Church missions have for a considerable time been conscious of the importance of keeping alive for as long as possible the aborigines' own art. More recently, in areas where there are large concentrations of aborigines still influenced by ancestral traditions, successful attempts have been made to introduce the aborigines' own art into the decoration of the Christian churches, and further interesting projects of this nature are planned. Under the guidance of the Reverend G. Armstrong, Methodist Chaplain at the Government Welfare Settlement at Maningrida, aboriginal artists are painting Christian subjects in their own traditional style.

The life expectancy of aboriginal art in its purely tribal form is strictly limited. It is inevitable that as wider horizons open for young aborigines, they no longer have the same intense interest in tribal traditions. Any attempt to prolong the life of tribal art when the inspiration for it is gone could only lead to its decline. The careful introduction of sacred subjects outside aboriginal tradition, while the art is still vital, may prove to be the means whereby aboriginal art can retain its vigour and beauty as tribal motivation diminishes.

In the Territories of Papua and New Guinea the adaptation of the indigenous arts to Christian use has followed a somewhat different course from that in Australia. European settlement has been of shorter duration, dating from the middle of the nineteenth century, and Europeans still form only a small proportion of the population. The country itself is extremely rugged, precipitous mountain ranges covered with dense tropical jungle making communication by land difficult. The people live in village communities in the mountain valleys, or in the steamy heat of the coastal areas, and there is little or no contact between neighbouring groups. Some of the people in the highlands districts, when first contacted by Europeans, were unaware of the existence of other human beings outside their own community.

Agriculture is the mainstay of life. Crops of taro, sweet potato or bananas are cultivated, and this diet is supplemented by the hunting of wild pigs and small game, or, in the case of the coastal people, by fishing. Houses and communal buildings are constructed, utilizing the materials most readily available, such as coconut palm, sago or black palm. The buildings vary greatly from district to district, both in design and craftmanship, ranging from very simple structures to the elaborately decorated spirit houses of the Sepik River area.

Arts and crafts, too, are greatly affected by the restricted communication; there is a great diversity in art styles, in the amount and quality of artistic expression, and also in the degree to which this is expressive of the mythology and beliefs of the people. While in some areas there is a great wealth of art—intricate wood and bone-carving, exotic masks and ceremonial art—in other areas one or two arts or crafts, such as the making of tapa cloth or grass skirts, constitute the sole artistic expression of the people.

In contrast to the missionaries in Australia, the Christian missionaries in Papua and New Guinea have been able from their first arrival, to adapt the local building styles to their needs, and have utilized the inexpensive buildings wherever possible, coconut matting helping to furnish the simple interiors. In recent years the decorative arts of the people have been incorporated more and more into the design and furnishings of the churches. In each district this presents an individual problem to the church involved, and great ingenuity is shown in using local arts and crafts to obtain the maximum effect. Where possible, the indigenous decoration is chosen for its appropriate significance, but some of the designs, though having some original traditional meaning, have been developed and used in a purely decorative manner, and are applied in this way to church decoration.

Most European Christian missionaries are very appreciative of the quality and importance of indigenous art, and discourage any deterioration of the artistic standards. Unfortunately many fine examples of church buildings and decoration in Papua and New Guinea no longer exist, as the materials used in their construction are not very durable in the humid climate.

Maori artists are making an important contribution to church decoration in New Zealand. The Maoris, Polynesian people who settled in New Zealand in the fourteenth century, had a great heritage of decorative art. After New Zealand came under British sovereignty in 1840, and Europeans settled throughout the Maori tribelands, arts and crafts were sadly depleted as the traditional way of life was disrupted and more and more people adapted themselves to European culture.

There are, however, a number of Maori craftsmen still skilled in the ancient arts and traditions, and their beautiful and intricate wood-carving, with its highly developed spiral and figure designs, and reed matting woven in traditional patterns, are being used with great effect and meaning both in church buildings and in Maori meeting houses, which are used for church services and social gatherings.

In New Zealand, as in Australia and New Guinea, the Christian church, by the use of indigenous arts, is not only helping to preserve ancient skills; it is at the same time drawing from them vitality and beauty, to the enrichment of church art.

2 *Stained glass window, Milingimbi Methodist Mission, Arnhem Land, depicting the cross in a setting of aboriginal totemic symbols. The window was made to a design by the Reverend E. A. Wells from colour photographs of clan symbols. Every part of the design is symbolic and has much meaning for the aboriginal people of the area*

3 *Nativity painting by Mick Magani of the Jinang tribe. Inside the cave Mary and Joseph are bending over the Baby Jesus. Also watching are some fellow tribesmen, some birds and a small kangaroo; some shrubs are growing close at hand. Outside the cave the wise men are travelling through rocky country to visit the child. Various types of trees and tubers (for food) are shown*

4 *Nativity painting by Bobby Baijjaray of the Maili tribe. The Baby Jesus can be seen on the paper-bark while Joseph and Mary in Mimi dress stand to the left. Hunters come with their dog to see the Child. Above, the Mimi angels are singing to the accompaniment of didgeridoo and clapsticks and one is announcing the good tidings. Their spears are laid in a bundle. A dreaming snake stands up; the black background and white spots on the left indicate night. Mimis are elongated 'stick' drawings of spirit figures occurring in certain parts of Arnhem Land*

5 *Nativity painting by Mick Magani. There is a double Nativity scene here showing Mary, Joseph and the Child Jesus in a rock shelter. Various types of trees stand nearby and small creatures have come near. Further away under the moon and stars a hunter is about to spear a big kangaroo. A goanna, wallaby and a small bird are in the bush there, too. Another man is holding aloft a ceremonial object, probably a 'morning star'*

6 *Nativity painting by Bilinyarra and Daingangan of Arnhem Land. In the bark shelter the artists have painted a number of babies wrapped in paper-bark and a man standing by with a spear in his hand. To the left are shepherds and a man in a high ceremonial hat and two stars. To the right are two people with various kinds of dilly-bag which are given as gifts. At the top of the painting is a large rock snake and a star*

2

3

4

5

6

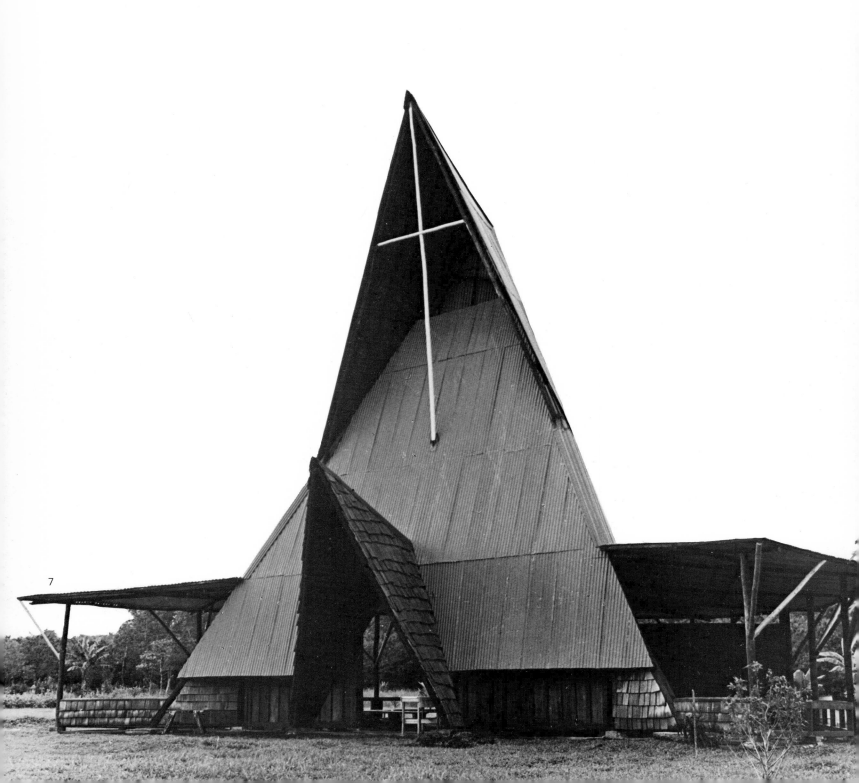

7 *Chapel at the Evangelists'
College, Jigarata, Papua, built in
the style of a Sepik Spirit House.
The house, Tamberan, or Spirit
House, in every Sepik village is
used as a men's club-house and a
place where sacred spirit figures
are kept*

7

8

8 'Our Lady of the Aborigines', Darwin Cathedral. Oil painting by Karol Kupka commissioned by Bishop O'Loughlin as a reminder that the message of Christianity is universal and to help bring religion to the people in terms of local understanding. The Holy Child is seated in typical aboriginal fashion on His Mother's shoulders. The background pattern is formed of totemic designs selected from bark paintings, cave drawings and artefacts

9 Church at Menapi built in the style of local houses using coconut leaves and bindoro posts; bindoro is a widely used hard wood. The interior has a floor of fine coral with coconut mats for kneeling. The altar frontal is made in the same way as the grass skirts of the area but dyed in different colours

9

10 *High altar, St Andrew's Church, Eroro, Papua. The figure of Christ the King is Papuan in style and the surrounding designs (traditional tapa cloth motifs), are painted on three-ply mounted over plaited bamboo. The altar frontal is painted store calico. The walls are made from central ribs of sago leaves, the candle-holders are insulators, relics from the Second World War, while the sanctuary lamp and gong are the bases of old Tilley lamps. The whole church is built on a concrete slab put down by the army*

11 *Movi Church, Eastern Highlands District, New Guinea. The people of this area build round houses with a pole protruding through the centre to keep away evil spirits. The church could not be built as a circle because of the size, but both ends were rounded to be in keeping with local building custom. Seven poles protruding through the roof symbolize the seven sacraments of the Church. The roof is very closely thatched and will last five to seven years*

12 *Chapel of the Native Community of the Visitation, Hetune, near Popondetta, Papua. The chapel was built by a friar of the Society of St Francis in a style based on the spirit houses of the Sepik River area. Materials used are galvanized iron and sago leaves, with a stone wall at the base*

13 *Church interior at Kumbun, New Britain. Kumbun is an island community and fishing plays a large part in the lives of the inhabitants. Fishing nets and paddles have been used for the altar surrounds and the early Christian symbol of the fish has added meaning here*

14 *Design by Margaret Haines for orphreys for a set of vestments. The Christian symbol for the sacrifice of Christ, the pelican pecking her breast to feed her young with drops of blood, is used in a style derived from aboriginal painting. Here the diamond shapes represent blood drops and the cross-hatching at the bottom, the nest*

15 *Bishop's throne, Dogura Cathedral, Papua. Tapa cloth has been used over wood. Over the central panel of tapa cloth is one of the insignia of chieftainship, presented to the Bishop by the Orokiava people when he was made Diocesan*

1
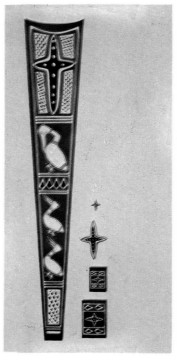

2

3

14

15

16 *Christ in the Korowai, St Faith's Anglican Church, Chinemutu, Rotorua, New Zealand. The Korowai is the cloak worn by a Maori chief; it is made with fibre and ornamented with kiwi feathers, with a taniko hem. Christ is pictured walking on Lake Rotorua. From the Lady Chapel*

17–19 *Tapa cloth cope made for the Primate of Australia, Archbishop Strong, when he was Bishop of New Guinea. Tapa cloth is made by women from the beaten bark of a type of wild mulberry and painted with vegetable colours in traditional family designs*

17

18

20–22 Bark panels painted for the decoration of the interior of the Catholic Mission Church, Ningil, Aitape, New Guinea. The panels show totemic designs which in the old traditions represent the connecting link between the spiritual world and earth. This church is in a very remote area where traditional beliefs still have a strong influence and Father Timothy gave the artists free rein in the decoration of the church

20

21

22

23 Wedding at Gona, Papua. Round her neck the bride is wearing the kambo, which was traditionally used in marriage ceremonies in this area in pre-Christian times. It has now been incorporated into the Anglican marriage service. During the ceremony the kambo is laid upon the altar and at the completion of the service it is placed round the bride's neck by her father

23

24–28 *Chapel of Turakina Maori Girls' College, Marton*

24 *Maori carving is most individualistic and only the carver can tell what the various carvings and markings symbolize. Unfortunately the professional carver of the the chapel has left no written record of his work and another carver has had to suggest what some of the designs could mean. Much of the work for the Chapel was done secretly, in accordance with Maori Tapu laws.*

25 *The lectern is made from totara wood and features a central panel of taniko work, a form of Maori tapestry in which natural dyed flax fibres are woven by hand. This is essentially women's work while carving is done solely by men. The spirals that feature in the carving depict the beginning of time and the continuation of life; the broken markings denote various phases of civilization; the carvings and the taniko work lead the eye upwards towards the large spiral.*

26 *The pulpit was carved in Rotorua under Tapu observances. The lattice or tukutuku work behind the pulpit depicts steps in the stairway to heaven. Kakaho reeds (toi-toi) are tied together to form a framework through which is woven the pingao (seashore grass) or flax. The tukutuku work on the pulpit shows the kaokao or armpit pattern. The wing-like pattern is symbolic of taking one under one's wing, or can be associated with the image or shelter, thereby fusing Maori and biblical worlds. The pulpit is supported on four teko-teko images. Before European settlement these supported the tohunga or priest's house.*

27 *The rafters and light bulbs are decorated with kowhaiwhai (scroll-work patterns) and features the traditional colours associated with the classical Maori art.*

28 *The stained glass window shows the Magi bringing gifts to the Holy Family. It is interesting to note that the Holy Family and one of the Magi are shown as Maoris*

GERVIS FRERE-COOK

THE TWENTIETH CENTURY

Perhaps historians of a hundred years hence may be able to look back and view the achievements and failures of the twentieth century objectively, but for the contemporary writer such an attitude is almost impossible. Within the last seventy years man has released for his own purposes the fantastic reservoirs of power stored within the earth since the beginning of time and the rate of his scientific and technological development is steadily increasing.

Inevitably therefore his attitude towards the universe is changing and his attitude towards God is undergoing drastic reappraisal. It may be correct to describe this century as the Century of Revolution, or the Era of Material Achievement, or even the Age of Instant Success; none of these apt phrases helps to answer the question, 'What is man and why is he here?' and its corollary, 'What happens after this life?' The problem today is that because we already know so much we think we must know everything, or at least be able to discover and comprehend the answer to every question, and religion is a mystery. Christianity above all is a religion of mysteries, the mysteries of the Incarnation and the Resurrection, without which it becomes meaningless. Yet the scientific humanist abhors mystery and demands a rational explanation for everything.

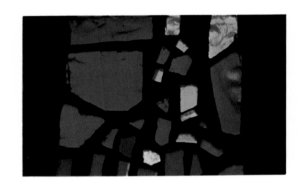

But once logic is unrestrained—and science is only the logical progression of experiment, observation and deduction—there is no limit to its processes nor the problems which it can presume to rationalize. The medieval churchmen may have been wiser than we know when they forced Galileo to deny his own writings. Not so long ago one of the world's leading atomic scientists withdrew himself from further research believing that mankind was trespassing beyond the proper bounds. Recent experiments in the fields of genetics and 'spare-part surgery' are causing other scientists to think deeply about the ethical justification of their work. There is the story of the physicist who switched on an immense computer and asked of it whether God existed. The reply was succinct: 'He does now.'

Likewise there has taken place throughout the world a great social revolution, not restricted to one or two countries but disseminated everywhere by the media of mass communication:

radio, television and the written word. A century ago that most Christian lady hymn-writer, Mrs C. F. Alexander, could in all sincerity pen the words:

> The rich man in his castle,
> The poor man at his gate;
> God made them high and lowly
> And ordered their estate.

and thousands of children's voices dutifully sang those words, never doubting that a social order so hallowed by God should be maintained. Two world wars and the rise of nationalism have changed such ideas and upset the nineteenth-century Christian attitude to God. No longer is He that benign Father-figure sitting on high, ruling the world through his royally anointed chosen upon earth, His Crown Prince Imperial sitting at His right hand; today men seek Truth with a capital 'T' (whatever they may think this to mean) and those with religious leanings concentrate on the humanity of Jesus Christ. Kindness and concern for others are the essential virtues of the age.

The tenets of the twentieth century, materialism, logic and efficiency, are reflected in the art and architecture of our time. Money and patronage which were once in the hands of the nobles are now controlled by directoral boards, anxious lest their shareholders accuse them of wasteful misuse of it; expenditure must be justified by a percentage return. The papal munificence which sponsored Michelangelo and Raphael is no more; no Lorenzo di Medici inspires the art of Birmingham or Boston. In an era of great affluence the Roman Catholic diocese of Liverpool had no easy task to raise the funds for its new Cathedral of Christ the King and at parochial level new housing estates rise churchless for lack of money. Seldom today do we build to the glory of God; today's Christianity feeds the hungry; vast international organizations with ships and aeroplanes now endeavour to do for millions what previously a few in holy orders did for hundreds. The emphasis has changed.

This change of emphasis has brought a change in the liturgy. Instead of the priest officiating at the altar at the far end of the church, acting as a go-between betwixt God and His people, new forms of service are being devised in contemporary language and churches are being built with the altar in the centre so that God is no longer confined to the sanctuary but comes down amongst the very congregation; following the example of the theatre the Church now offers 'communion in the round' and encourages audience participation. And why not, since Christianity declares that all men are equal in the sight of God while modern socialism goes even further and avers that all men are equal everywhere!

How then has all this affected Christian art? In painting and sculpture artists have been moved to portray the humanity of Christ in contemporary terms, works such as Stanley Spencer's 'Christ Preaching at Cookham Reach' and John Bratby's 'Crucifixion' which, when exhibited, aroused great controversy and in less liberal times would no doubt have caused their creators to be sadly persecuted. In Africa and India pictures have been painted of Christ with a black skin. But generally such paintings are realistic in style; Christian themes seem to have little appeal for the impressionist or surrealist artist and abstract art rarely suggests a religious inspiration.

But architecture has caught the spirit of the century despite the paucity of monumental building. Inspired by the genius of Frank Lloyd Wright and Le Corbusier, the twentieth-century architects have exploited the technical achievements of the age: reinforced concrete, stressed steel girders, extruded aluminium, sheets of plate glass, all these have been used to design and build in a way which was previously impossible. In a world which is reaching for the stars—and has already arrived at the moon—God can no longer be hidden up there just behind the clouds. He must be out there in space, infinite and everlasting, and the anthropomorphic approach must be discarded. So, while the pictures of today define the humanity of Christ, the buildings of today seek to show the infinity of God. Space and light, form and void, vastness and detail: decoration is eschewed for proportion and suggestion, for light and shadow. Consider the 'praying hands' roof of Lundy's Unitarian Church, Westport, Connecticut, or the aerofoil shape of the US Air Force Chapel at Colorado Springs. Look at the use of plain glass and light in Perret's Church of St Joseph, Le Havre, and the riotously coloured panes of Corbusier's Ronchamp and Spence's rebuilt Coventry Cathedral. Reflect on the wonder of Nature as seen through the altar window at Otaniemi. Surely the message of the twentieth-century architects is clear: 'God is a spirit and they that worship Him must worship Him in spirit.'

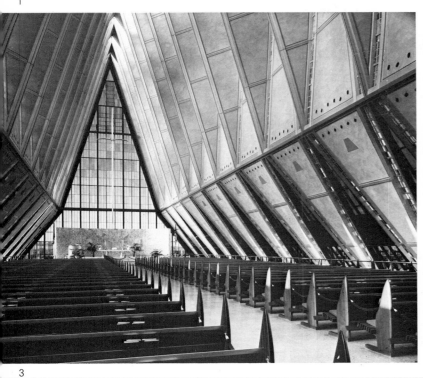

8

4–7 *Wayfarers' Chapel,*
Portuguese Bend, California.
(Frank Lloyd Wright)

8 *Sagrada Familia, Barcelona.*
Gaudi's unique unfinished
masterpiece

9

10

11

12

9 *Altar and cross of the Technical Students Chapel, Otaniemi, Finland. (The Sirens)*

10 *Exterior approach at Otaniemi*

11, 12 *Interior and exterior of Notre Dame de Royan. (Gillet)*

13, 14 *Interior and exterior, chapel at Ronchamp. (Le Corbusier)*

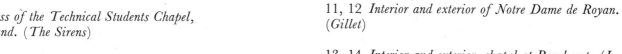

13

14

15, 16 *Interior and exterior, parish church of St Rendentore, Turin. (Nicola Mosso)*

17 *The framework of the cathedral at Brasilia whilst under construction (Oscar Niemeyer). The same motif of the Crown of Glory has been used in the Roman Catholic Cathedral of Christ the King, Liverpool*

18 *Chapel of Our Lady of Solitude, Coyoacan, Mexico City. (Felix Candela)*

19 20

19, 20 *Interior and exterior, Unity Church, Oak Park, Illinois.* (Frank Lloyd Wright)

21 *Church of Our Lady of Fatima, Lisbon*

22 *Färsta Church, Stockholm*

23 *Madonna and Child.* (Epstein)

21

23

22

24

25

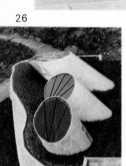

26

27

28

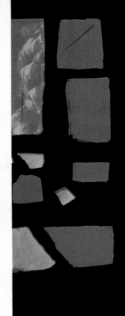

24–29 *The Monastery of L'Arbresle.*
(*Le Corbusier*)

24 *The south-west façade*

25 *The high altar seen from the congregation*

26 *Corner of the roof, north façade*

27 *View from the monks' choir*

28 *Interior of the crypt*

29 *Altar of the Holy Sacrament in the crypt*

29

32

33

34

35

36

30–32 *Stained glass in the Kaiser Wilhelm Memorial Church, Berlin. (Errman)*

33 *Interior of Church of Notre-Dame de Raincy, St. Denis, Paris. (Perret)*

34 *Church of St Joseph, Le Havre. (Perret)*

35 *Crucifix, Vence Chapel. (Matisse)*

36 *The font and Piper Window in the Baptistry, Coventry Cathedral. (Basil Spence)*

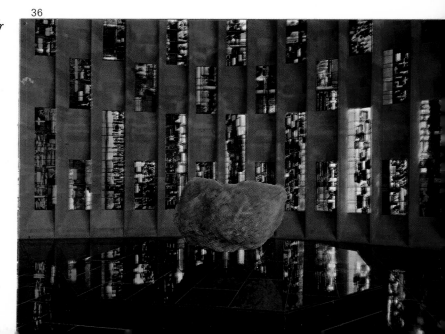

37

38

39

40

41

The copyright in the contributions to this book is as follows:

PRELUDE: THE ART OF THE JEWS © Joseph Gutmann 1972
THE FIRST PORTRAYAL © Joan Morris 1972
MONASTERY AND CATHEDRAL © E. R. Chamberlin 1972
THE EASTERN ORTHODOX CHURCH © John Innes 1972
ROME AND THE RENAISSANCE © J. Holland-Smith 1972
ENGLAND AFTER THE REFORMATION © Eric R. Delderfield 1972
NORTH OF THE BALTIC © Martin Blindheim 1972
BAROQUE AND ROCOCO © Peter Cannon-Brookes 1972
REVIVAL IN RUSSIA © Michael Bourdeaux 1972
THE CHURCH IN NORTH AMERICA © Robert Sefton 1972
THE CHURCH IN SOUTH AMERICA © Cottie A. Burland 1972
MISSION IN AFRICA © Margaret Hubbard 1972
INDIA AND THE FAR EAST © John F. Butler 1972
THE ISLANDS AND AUSTRALASIA © Margaret Haines 1972
THE TWENTIETH CENTURY © Gervis Frere-Cook 1972

The Editor wishes to express his appreciation for permission to reproduce the illustrations in this book granted by the various Owners, Trustees, Directors or other administrative bodies listed below, and his thanks to those who have helped collect the illustrations, particularly Illustration Research Service, London, for without such help the book could never have been produced.

Frontispiece
Dean and Chapter, Gloucester Cathedral

Chapter 1
Damascus Museum: 1 3 5 9
Biblioteca Apostolica, Vatican: 2 12
Bibliothèque Nationale, Paris: 4 6 15
Palphot, Jerusalem: 7
British Museum, London: 10
Leningrad Museum: 8
Bibliothèque Municipale, Amiens: 11
Alinari/Mansell: 13
Nationalbibliothek, Vienna: 14

Chapter 2
Anderson: 1
Alinari: 2 9 10
Musée de Bardo, Tunisia: 3 7 16
Pontificia Commissione di Archaelogia Sacra, Rome: 4 8 19 20
Metropolitan Museum of Art, N.Y.: 5
Alinari/Mansell: 6 25 27
John Innes: 11 12
Staatsbibliothek, Munich: 13
Vatican Museum: 14 30
Damascus Museum: 15
British Museum, London: 17 18 22 29
U.N.E.S.C.O., Paris: 21 28
Coptic Museum, Cairo: 23
Richter: 24
Opera del Duomo, Monza: 26
Courtauld Institute of Art, London: 31

Chapter 3
Alinari/Mansell: 1
Giraudon/Mansell: 2 5 9 10 12
Courtauld Institute of Art, London: 3 14 32
Bibliothèque Nationale, Paris: 4 15
Alinari: 6 7 8 11 13
Trinity College, Cambridge: 16
Helga Schmidt-Glassner: 17 20
Bundesdenkmalamt, Vienna: 18
Giraudon: 19
Nationalbibliothek, Vienna: 21
Pierpont Morgan Library, N.Y.: 22
British Museum, London: 23 27
Bibliothèque Municipale, Amiens: 24
Anderson/Mansell: 25
Rheinisch Bildarchiv, Cologne: 26
French Government Tourist Office: 28 29
Mansell: 30 31   Bernard Cox: 33
Bodleian Library, Oxford: 34 35

Chapter 4
A. F. Kersting: 1
Hi-Fi Colour Slides: 2 33 52
Alinari/Mansell: 3
Courtauld Institute of Art, London: 4
Victor Kennett: 10 32 57 58
Monastère Chevtogne, Belgium: 16 17
Bernard Cox: 18
Dubrovnik Orthodox Museum: 24
R. F. Hoddinott: 35   Mansell: 41
John Innes and Basil Minchin: all others

Chapter 5
Alinari: 1 2 3 4 7 8 10 13 14 15 16 17 19 38
Wallace Collection, London: 5
Anderson: 6 11 24 25 31
Brogi: 9 18
National Gallery, London: 12 29
Mansell: 20
Musée du Louvre, Paris: 21 22 23 26 27 28 33 34
Anderson/Mansell: 30
National Gallery of Art, Washington D.C.: 32
Alinari/Mansell: 35
Victoria and Albert Museum, London: 36 37 39

Chapter 6
E.R.D. Publications, Exmouth: all illustrations

Chapter 7
National Archaeological Museum, Reykjavik: 1
National Museum, Copenhagen: 2
Nationalmuseet Kildeangivelse: 3 7 10 11 12 17 18 23 24
Universitetets Oldsaksamling, Oslo: 4 5 6 13 14 15
Historisk Museum, Bergen: 8 16
Riksantikvaren, Oslo: 9 20
National Museum, Finland: 19 21
Lennart Olson: 22 25